Ernst Wolff

Pillaging the World

The History and Politics of the IMF

tectum

Ernst Wolff

Pillaging the World

The History and Politics of the IMF

Tectum

Ernst Wolff

Pillaging the World.
The History and Politics of the IMF

Image credits book cover: gun © runningbean / www.istockphoto.com;
Earth seen from *Apollo 17,* photographer: Harrison Schmitt or Ron Evans,
December 7, 1972.
© Tectum Verlag Marburg, 2014
ISBN 978-3-8288-3438-5
Druck und Bindung: Schaltungsdienst Lange

Please visit us at our website:
www.tectum-verlag.de

This book is dedicated to those people in Africa, Asia and South America who cannot read it because the politics of the IMF have denied them the right to education.

Contents

Foreword

No other financial organization has affected the lives of the majority of the world's population more profoundly over the past fifty years than the *International Monetary Fund* (IMF). Since its inception after World War II, it has expanded its sphere of influence to the remotest corners of the earth. Its membership currently includes 188 countries on five continents.

For decades, the IMF has been active mainly in Africa, Asia and South America. There is hardly a country on these continents where its policies have not been carried out in close cooperation with the respective national governments. When the global financial crisis broke out in 2007, the IMF turned its attention to northern Europe. Since the onset of the Euro crisis in 2009, its primary focus has shifted to southern Europe.

Officially, the IMF's main task consists in stabilizing the global financial system and helping out troubled countries in times of crisis. In reality, its operations are more reminiscent of warring armies. Wherever it intervenes, it undermines the sovereignty of states by forcing them to implement measures that are rejected by the majority of the population, thus leaving behind a broad trail of economic and social devastation.

In pursuing its objectives, the IMF never resorts to the use of weapons or soldiers. It simply applies the mechanisms of capitalism, specifically those of credit. Its strategy is as simple as it is effective: When a country runs into financial difficulties, the IMF steps in and provides support in the form of loans. In return, it demands the enforcement of measures that serve to ensure the country's solvency in order to enable it to repay these loans.

Because of its global status as "lender of last resort" governments usually have no choice but to accept the IMF's offer and submit to its terms – thus getting caught in a web of debt, which they, as a result of interest, compound interest and principal, get deeper and deeper entangled in. The resulting strain on the state budget and the domestic economy inevitably leads to a deterioration of their financial situation, which the IMF in turn uses as a pretext for demanding ever new concessions in the form of "austerity programs".

The consequences are disastrous for the ordinary people of the countries affected (which are mostly low-income) because their governments all follow the same pattern, passing the effects of austerity on to wage earners and the poor.

In this manner, IMF programs have cost millions of people their jobs, denied them access to adequate health care, functioning educational systems and decent housing. They have rendered their food unaffordable, increased homelessness, robbed old people of the fruits of lifelong work, favored the spread of diseases, reduced life expectancy and increased infant mortality.

At the other end of the social scale, however, the policies of the IMF have helped a tiny layer of ultra-rich increase their vast fortunes even in times of crisis. Its measures have contributed decisively to the fact that global inequality has assumed historically unprecedented levels. The income difference between a sun king and a beggar at the end of the Middle Ages pales compared to the difference between a hedge fund manager[1] and a social welfare recipient of today.

---

[1] In 2010 hedge fund manager John Paulsen earned $ 5 billion. This equals a daily income of $ 19.2 million, almost ten million times the amount of $ 2 a

Although these facts are universally known and hundreds of thousands have protested the effects of its measures in past decades, often risking their lives, the IMF tenaciously clings on to its strategy. Despite all criticism and despite the strikingly detrimental consequences of its actions, it still enjoys the unconditional support of the governments of all leading industrial nations.

Why? How can it be that an organization that causes such immense human suffering around the globe continues to act with impunity and with the backing of the most powerful forces of our time? In whose interest does the IMF work? Who benefits from its actions?

It is the purpose of this book to answer these questions.

---

day which 2.5 billion people had to live on that year.

Harry Dexter White and John Maynard Keynes at the opening meeting of the IMF's Board of Governors in Savannah, Georgia, March 8, 1946.

The Bretton Woods Conference:
Starting out with Blackmail

While the Second World War was still raging in Europe, in July 1944, the United States invited delegations from 44 countries to the small ski resort of Bretton Woods, New Hampshire. The official aim of the conference, held for three weeks in the luxurious "Mount Washington" hotel, was to define the basic features of an economic order for the post-war period and to provide the cornerstones of a system that would stabilize the world economy and prevent a return to the situation that had existed between the two world wars. The 1930s in particular were distinguished by high inflation, trade barriers, strongly fluctuating exchange rates, gold shortages and a decline in economic activity by more than 60 %. Furthermore, social tensions had constantly threatened to break down the established order.

The conference had been preceded by several years of secret negotiations between the White House and Downing Street which had already been working on plans for a new world monetary order since 1940. A recorded comment from the head of the British delegation, the economist Lord Keynes, sheds light on the former elite's attitude towards the interests and concerns of smaller countries: "Twenty-one countries have been invited which clearly have nothing to contribute and will merely encumber the ground... The most monstrous monkeyhouse assembled for years."[2]

---

[2] Richard Peet, "Unholy Trinity", ZED Books, 2009

It did not take long before their contemptuous attitude rebounded on Lord Keynes and his compatriots. During the course of the conference, it became increasingly clear how much the global balance of power had shifted to the disadvantage of Great Britain. Excessive war spending had turned the country, already severely weakened by the First World War, into the world's biggest debtor and pushed it to the brink of insolvency. Great Britain's economy was on its knees and the rise of the liberation movements around the world already heralded the final breakup of its once global colonial empire.

The undisputed victor of the Second World War, however, was the United States. Having become the largest international creditor, it held nearly two-thirds of the world's gold reserves and commanded half of all global industrial production. In contrast to most European countries its infrastructure was intact and while its delegation engaged in negotiations at Bretton Woods, the US army's general staff planned a nuclear assault on the Japanese cities of Hiroshima and Nagasaki in order to emphasize America's claim to global dominion.

As a result of this new balance of power, Lord Keynes' plan for a new economic order was flatly rejected. Representing a country with substantial balance of payments problems, he had proposed an "international payments union" that would have given countries suffering from a negative balance of payments easier access to loans and introduced an international accounting unit called "Bancor" which would have served as a reserve currency.

The US, however, was unwilling to take on the role of a major creditor that Keynes' plan had foreseen for it. The leader of their delegation, economist Harry Dexter White, in turn presented his own plan that was finally adopted by the conference. This "White Plan" conceptualized a world currency system never before seen in the history of money. The US dollar was to constitute its sole center and was to be pegged to all other currencies at a fixed exchange rate while its exchange relation to gold was to be set at $ 35 per ounce of fine gold. The plan was supplemented by US demands for the establishment of several international organizations designed to monitor the new system and stabilize it by granting loans to countries facing balance of payments problems.

After all, Washington, due to its size and rapid economic growth, had to move ahead in order to obtain access to raw materials and create global sales opportunities for its overproduction. This required replacing the hitherto most widely used currency, the British pound, by the dollar. Also, time seemed ripe for replacing the City of London by Wall Street, thus establishing the US in its new position as the focal point of international trade and global finance.

The gold-dollar peg and the establishment of fixed exchange rates partially reintroduced the gold standard, which had existed between 1870 and the outbreak of World War I – albeit under very different circumstances. By fixing all exchange rates to the US dollar, Washington deprived all other participating countries of the right to control their own monetary policy for the protection of their domestic industries – a first step towards curtailing the sovereignty of the rest of the world by the now dominant United States.

The distribution of voting rights suggested by the US for the proposed organizations[3] was also far from democratic. Member countries were not to be treated equally or assigned voting rights according to the size of their population, but rather corresponding to the contributions they paid – which meant that Washington, by means of its financial superiority, secured itself absolute control over all decisions. The fact that South Africa's racist apartheid dictatorship was invited to become

---

[3] Aside from founding the IMF, the Bretton Woods conference also decided to set up its sister organization World Bank, which was initially called „International Bank for reconstruction and development". It took up operations by granting loans for reconstruction projects following the devastation of World War II.

a founding member of the IMF sheds a revealing light on the role that humanitarian considerations played in the process.

The US government sensed that it would not be easy to win over public opinion for a project so obviously in contradiction with the spirit of the US constitution and many Americans' understanding of democracy. The true goals of the IMF were therefore obfuscated with great effort and glossed over by empty rhetoric about "free trade" and the "abolition of protectionism". The *New York Herald-Tribune* spoke of the "most high-powered propaganda campaign in the history of the country."

The IMF's first task was to scrutinize all member states in order to determine their respective contribution rates. After all, the Fund was to exert a long-term "monitoring" function for the system's protection. The US thus claimed for itself the right to be permanently informed about the financial and economic conditions of all countries involved.

When half a year after the conference the British insisted on an improvement in their favor to the contracts, they were unambiguously made aware of who was in charge of the IMF. Without further ado Washington tied a loan of $ 3.75 billion, urgently needed by the U.K. to repay its war debts, to the condition that Great Britain submit to the terms of the agreement without any ifs, ands, or buts. Less than two weeks later Downing Street gave in to Washington's blackmail and consented.

On December 27, 1945, 29 governments signed the final agreement. In January 1946, representatives of 34 nations came together for an introductory meeting of the Board of Governors of the IMF and the World Bank in Savannah, Georgia. On this occasion, Lord Keynes and his compatriots were once again left empty-handed: Contrary to their proposal to establish the headquarters of the IMF, which had in the meantime been declared a specialized agency of the United Nations, in New York City, the US government insisted on its right to determine the location solely by itself. On March 1, 1947, the IMF finally took up its operations in downtown Washington.

The rules for membership in the IMF were simple: Applicant countries had to open their books and were rigorously screened and assessed. After that they had to deposit a certain amount of gold and pay their financial contribution to the organization according to their economic power. In return, they were assured that in the case of balance of payments problems they were entitled to a credit up to the extent of their contribution – in exchange for interest rates determined by the IMF and the contractually secured obligation of settling their debts to the IMF before all others.

The IMF finally received a starting capital of $ 8.8 billion from shares of its member states who paid 25 % of their contributions in gold and 75 % in their own currency. The United States secured itself the highest rate by depositing $ 2.9 billion. The amount was twice as high as Great Britain's and guaranteed the United States not only double voting rights, but also a blocking minority and veto rights.

The IMF was run by a Board of Governors, to whom twelve executive directors were subordinated. Seven were elected by the members of the IMF, the other five were appointed by the largest countries, led by the US. The offices of the IMF as well as those of its sister organization, the World Bank, were set up on Pennsylvania Avenue in Washington within walking distance from the White House.

The original statutes of the IMF state that the organization's objectives were, among others,

- To promote international cooperation in the field of monetary policy,

- To facilitate the expansion and balanced growth of international trade,

- To promote exchange rate stability and assist in the establishment of a multilateral system of payments,

- To provide member countries facing balance of payments difficulties with temporary access to the Fund's general resources and under adequate safeguards,

- To shorten the duration and lessen the degree of disequilibrium in the international balances of payments of member countries.

These official terms make it seem as if the IMF is an impartial institution, placed above nations and independent of political influences, its main objective consisting in running the global economy in as orderly a manner as possible, swiftly correcting malfunctions. This is no coincidence. This impression was intended by the authors and has in fact achieved its desired effect: It is exactly this notion that has been conveyed to the global public for more than six decades by politicians, scientists and the international media.

In actual fact, the IMF has, from the very beginning, been an institution launched by, controlled by, and tailored to the interests of the United States, designed to secure the new military superpower economic world domination. To con-

ceal these intentions even more effectively, the founding fathers of the IMF in 1947 started a tradition which the organization has held to this day – appointing a non-American to the post of managing director.

The first foreigner, selected in 1946, was Camille Gutt from Belgium. As finance minister of his country during World War II, the trained economist had helped the British cover

Camille Gutt in Bretton Woods, 1944

their war expenses by lending them Belgian gold. He had aided the war effort by supplying his government's allies with cobalt and copper from the Belgian colony of Congo and supporting the US government with secret deliveries of Congolese uranium for its nuclear program. In 1944 he had carried out a drastic currency reform (later known as the "Gutt operation") that had cost the working population of Belgium large amounts of their savings.

Gutt headed the IMF from 1946 to 1951. During his time in office he largely focused on the implementation and monitoring of fixed exchange rates, thus ushering in a new era of hitherto unknown stability for US and international corporations when exporting goods and purchasing raw materials. He also paved the way for major US banks seeking to deal in credits on an international scale and opened up markets all over the world for international finance capital searching for investment opportunities.

The world's major political changes after World War II caused considerable headaches for the IMF, because they limited the scope of the organization. Above all, the Soviet Union took advantage of the post-war situation, characterized by the division of the world among the major powers and the drawing of new borders in Europe. Still relying on the socialization of the means of production by the Russian Revolution of 1917, Stalin's officials sealed off the so-called "Eastern bloc" from the West in order to introduce central economic planning in these countries. The Soviet bureaucracy's primary objective, however, was not to enforce the interests of working people, but to assure the subordination of the Eastern Bloc under its own interests for the purpose of pillaging these countries[4]. In any case, the fragmentation of Eastern Europe meant that Poland, East Germany, Czechoslovakia,

---

[4] After the division of Germany into zones of occupation, large parts of East Germany's productive capacities were "dismantled". Between 1945 and 1948 the Soviet Union removed, among others, four-fifths of the car industry and three-quarters of the steel industry from its zone.

Hungary, Romania, Bulgaria and several other markets became blank areas for international financial capital.

20 The seizure of power by Mao Zedong in 1949 and the introduction of a planned economy in China by the Communist Party deprived Western investors of another huge market and eventually led to the Korean War. Implementing their policy of "containment" of the Soviet Union's sphere of influence, the US tacitly accepted the loss of four million lives only to deliver a clear message to the rest of the world: that the largest economic power on earth would no longer remain passive if denied access to any more global markets.

The Post-War Boom: The IMF Casts its Net

The post-war years were characterized by the rapid economic growth of all leading industrial nations, referred to as the "Wirtschaftswunder" ("economic miracle") in Germany. Although IMF lending played only a minor role during this time, the organization's leadership did not remain inactive. On the contrary: the second IMF chief Ivar Rooth, a former Governor of the Swedish Central Bank and ex-Director of the Basel *Bank for International Settlements*[5], set out on a course that was to acquire major significance in

Ivar Rooth (1888–1972)

the later history of the organization – introducing conditionality, i.e. establishing obligatory requirements for granting loans.

Harry Dexter White had already made a proposal along these lines at the Bretton Woods Conference, but encountered fierce resistance from the British. Meanwhile, however, Britain's position had continued to deteriorate. Former colonies, mainly in Africa, were fighting for their independence, and in the Middle East the Suez crisis[6] was

---

[5] Umbrella organization of national central banks
[6] After Egypt's nationalization of the Suez Canal, Britain and France, supported by Israel, intervened militarily, but were forced by the US and the Soviet Union to conclude a ceasefire.

looming – providing the US with an opportunity to advance its own interests in the IMF more forcefully.

By establishing so-called "stand-by arrangements", Ivar Rooth added the principle of "conditionality" to the IMF's toolbox. The granting of loans was now subjected to conditions that went far beyond the specification of loan deadlines and the level of interest rates.

In implementing these measures, which were tightened after Britain's defeat in Suez led to a rise of tensions in Anglo-American relations, the IMF's strategists developed a strategy that helped them to cleverly deceive the public. Starting in 1958, they obliged the governments of debtor countries to draw up "letters of intent" in which they had to express their willingness to undertake "reasonable efforts" to master their balance of payments problems. This made it seem as though a country had itself proposed the measures that were actually required by the IMF.

But even that did not go far enough for the IMF. As a next step, loans to be disbursed were sliced into tranches ("phasing") and thus made conditional upon the respective debtor country's submissiveness. In addition, the IMF insisted (and still insists) that agreements between the IMF and its debtors should not be considered international treaties and therefore should not be subject to parliamentary approval. Finally, the IMF decreed that any agreements with it were not intended for the public eye and had to be treated as classified information – a scheme that applies to this day.

Conditions were to be continually tightened in the course of the IMF's history and would prove to be a crucial mechanism for increasing foreign domination of developing countries. They also contributed to the growing power of the IMF, because the World Bank, most governments and the vast majority of international commercial banks from now on only granted loans to those countries which, on the basis of the fulfillment of the IMF's criteria, had received its "seal of approval".

In 1956 a meeting was held in Paris that was to win landmark importance for the later development of the IMF. Struggling to repay a loan, Argentina had to sit down with its creditor countries and representatives of the IMF in order to have new conditions dictated to it. The meeting took place in the offices of French Finance Minister Pierre Pflimlin, who also chaired it. It did not remain the only one of its kind. In subsequent years, meetings between IMF representatives, creditors and debtors were held frequently in the same place, gradually developing into fixed monthly conferences that were to become known as the "Paris Club". A scope of extremely important decisions were taken within this framework – without parliamentary consent and hidden from the eyes of the public. Commercial banks around the world soon recognized the importance of these conferences, and therefore started their own "London Club", whose meetings usually took (and still take) place simultaneously with those of the Paris Club.

Barely noticed by the global community, the IMF subsequently turned to a field of activity that was to boost its power massively in a relatively short time. The wave of declarations of independence by African states at the beginning of the 1960s[7] marked the beginning of a new era. Countries that had been plundered for decades by colonialism and lay in tatters economically, now had to find their proper place in the world and especially in the world economy under rapidly changing conditions. Their governments therefore needed money. Since most of these countries offered commercial banks too little security due to social tensions, political unrest and barely existing infrastructure, the IMF took advantage of the situation and offered its services as a creditor.

Although most African countries were so poor that they were only granted relatively modest sums, even these had consequences. The ma-

23

---

[7]   1960 is called the "African year", because 18 former colonies (14 of them French, two British, one Belgian and one Italian) declared their independence that year.

turity dates of interest and principal payments relentlessly ensured that states that had just escaped from colonial dependence were seamlessly caught in a new network of financial dependence on the IMF.

As credit lending required the debtor's membership in the IMF, the organization, whose founding members had only included three African countries – Egypt, Ethiopia, and South Africa – was joined by more than 40 additional African states between 1957 and 1969. In 1969, 44 out of 115 members were African. Although they made up more than one third of the overall organization, their voting rights that same year amounted to less than 5 %.

Chile 1973:
Embarking upon the Path of Neoliberalism

The beginning of the 1970s marked the end of the post-war boom, a twenty-five year period of economic expansion in which workers in the leading industrial nations had been granted great social concessions and experienced a hitherto unknown improvement of their living standards. It was the internal disintegration of the Bretton Woods system that brought about the end of that period. As a result of rising US investment abroad and escalating military spending – particularly for the Vietnam War – the amount of dollars globally in circulation had continually increased. All attempts by the US government to bring this proliferation under control had failed because US capital had blended with foreign capital and no nation on earth was capable of reining in this massive concentration of financial power.

In 1971, the United States, for the first time in its history, ran a balance of payments deficit. At the same time the imbalance between the global dollar supply and US gold reserves stored in Fort Knox assumed such dimensions that even raising the gold price to $ 38.00 and then to $ 42.20 could no longer guarantee its exchange against an ounce of gold.[8] On August 15, 1971, US President Nixon pulled the brakes and

---

[8]   The amount of dollars circulating outside the USA increased from $ 5 billion a year in 1951 to $ 38,5 billion in 1968, thus exceeding US gold reserves by $ 23 billion.

severed the link between gold and the dollar, displaying the typical arrogance of a superpower by not consulting a single ally.[9]

In December 1971, a conference of the G10 group, founded in 1962 by the world's top ten industrialized nations, decided on an alignment of exchange rates, which brought about a readjustment of the dollar's value against other currencies. This led to a devaluation of the dollar, ranging from 7.5 % against the weak Italian lira to 16.9 % against the strong Japanese yen. In February 1973, the dollar was devalued again, but it soon became clear that the system of fixed exchange rates could no longer be upheld. In March 1973, the G10 and several other industrialized countries introduced the system of flexible exchange rates to be established by the central banks – without consulting a single country outside the G 10 and despite the fact that the new regime blatantly contradicted article 6 of the founding document of the IMF on fixed exchange rates and monetary stability.

The abolition of fixed exchange rates historically terminated the core tasks of the IMF. The only role left for it was that of a lender in charge of the allocation of funds and their conditionality, entitled to inspect the accounts of applicants and thus exercise direct influence on their policies. However, it was exactly this function for which extremely favorable conditions would soon arise.

In 1973, the members of the *Organization of the Petroleum Exporting Countries* (OPEC), which had been founded in 1960, used the Yom Kippur War between Egypt and Israel to curb the amount of oil supplied to the West ("oil embargo") and drastically raise oil prices. This led to a huge increase in the profits of oil companies and oil-producing countries. These gains ended up in commercial banks, which in turn tried to use them for profitable investments. As the global economy slipped into a recession in 1974/75 and investment opportunities in

---

[9]   It was only minutes before Nixon's televised speech that Pierre-Paul Schweitzer, then president of the IMF, was informed about Washington's decision.

industrialized countries dwindled, the lion's share of the money took on the form of loans to third world countries in Asia, Africa and South America, which – due to their increased expenditures after the rise in oil prices – urgently needed money. The IMF itself responded to the increased credit needs of developing countries by introducing the "Extended Fund Facility" in 1974, from which member countries could draw loans of up to 140 % of their quota with terms of four and a half to ten years.

Although the facility had been specifically set up to finance much-needed oil imports, the IMF – as well as the banks – cared little about what the money was actually spent on. Whether it went straight into the pockets of dictators such as Mobutu in Zaire[10], Saddam Hussein in Iraq or Suharto in Indonesia – who either squandered it, transferred it to secret foreign accounts or used it for military purposes, in each case driving up the national debt – did not matter to the IMF and the banks as long as they received their interest payments regularly.

However, the situation changed abruptly when Paul Volcker, the new chairman of the US Federal Reserve, raised its prime rate (the interest rate at which commercial banks can obtain money from central banks) by 300 % in order to reduce inflation in 1979. The United States slipped into another recession, which meant that fewer raw materials were needed due to lower economic activity.

For many developing countries the combination of receding demand, falling raw material prices and skyrocketing interest rates meant that they could not meet their payment obligations to international banks. A massive financial crisis loomed. The debt burden of developing countries at the beginning of 1980 amounted to a total of $ 567 billion. A

---

[10] During his reign dictator Mobutu succeeded in accumulating $ 12 billion in public debt and $ 4 billion in private assets. Saddam Hussein managed to obtain $162 billion in loans, using them for building palaces, expanding his repressive apparatus and waging wars against Iran und Kuwait.

payment default of this magnitude would have led to the collapse of many Western banks and therefore had to be prevented at all costs.

28   It was at this point that the IMF was given its first great chance to enter the stage as a lender of last resort. While its public relations department spread the news that the organization was working on bail-outs in order to "help" over-indebted countries, the Fund took advantage of its incontestable monopoly position and tied the granting of loans to harsh conditions. In doing so, it was able to draw on two different experiences gained in the preceding years.

Firstly, a CIA-supported military coup in Chile in September 1973 had ended socialist president Salvador Allende's rule and brought fascist dictator Augusto Pinochet to power. Pinochet had immediately reversed Allende's nationalizations, but found no remedy against galloping inflation. In an attempt to regain control of the situation, he had turned to a group of 30 Chilean economists (known as the "Chicago Boys" because they had studied at the Chicago School of Economics under Nobel Prize winner Milton Friedman) and proposed to them a clearly defined division of labor: He would provide for the suppression of any kind of political and trade union opposition and crush all labor disputes, while they were to carry out a radical austerity program on the basis of neoliberal[11] ideas.

Within a few weeks an extensive catalog of measures was developed. It called for a drastic limitation of money supply, cuts in government spending, layoffs in the public sector, privatization in health care and education, wage cuts and tax increases for working people, while at the same time lowering tariffs and corporate taxes. The program was openly referred to as a "shock therapy" by either side.

---

[11] "Neoliberalism", the dominant ideology of international finance capital since the early 1970s, calls for the state to stay out of the economy and leave its regulation largely to the markets. By contrast, "Keynesianism" demands that the state actively intervene in the economy in times of crisis.

Augusto Pinochet meeting with US Secretary of State Henry Kissinger, 1976

Both Pinochet and his partners, who were presented to the public as a "government of technocrats", fulfilled their side of the agreement to the hilt. While the dictator violently smashed any opposition to the government's drastic measures and ensured that many political dissidents disappeared forever, the "Chicago Boys" launched a frontal assault on the working population. They drove up unemployment, which had stood at 3 % in 1973, to 18.7 % by the end of 1975, simultaneously pushing inflation to 341 % and plunging the poorest segments of the population into even deeper poverty. The impacts of the program actually aggravated the problem of social inequality for decades to come: In 1980, the richest 10 % of the Chilean population amassed 36.5 % of the national income, expanding their share to 46.8 % in 1989, while at the same time that of the poorest 50 % fell from 20.4 % to 16.8 %.

During his bloody coup, Pinochet had fully relied on the active support of the CIA and the US Department of State under Henry Kissinger. When implementing the toughest austerity program ever carried out in a Latin American country, the "Chicago Boys" received the full backing of the IMF. Regardless of all human rights violations, IMF loans to Chile doubled in the year after Pinochet's coup, only to quadruple and quintuple in the following two years.

The IMF's other experience concerned the UK. Great Britain's inexorable economic decline over two and a half decades had made the country the IMF's largest borrower. From 1947 to 1971, the government in London had drawn loans totaling $ 7.25 billion. After the recession of 1974 / 75 and speculative attacks on the pound, it had come under even greater pressure. When in 1976, the British government once again turned to the IMF for help, the United States seized the opportunity to demonstrate their power. Allying themselves with the resurgent Germans, they forced the Labour government under Prime Minister Harold Wilson to limit public spending, impose massive cuts in social programs, pursue a restrictive fiscal policy, and refrain from import controls of any kind. This drastic intervention represented a hitherto unknown encroachment on the sovereignty of a European borrower country, resulting in the fact that no leading Western industrialized country ever again applied for an IMF loan.

Laying out a Course of Action:
The IMF's "Structural Adjustment Programs"

The events in Chile and Great Britain made the IMF leadership realize that it was time to adjust its agenda to its new role as a pioneer of neoliberal reforms, paving the way for US finance capital in developing countries. This was done in two steps in 1978 and 1979.

In April 1978, the statutes of the IMF were amended, introducing the items of "financial support", "technical assistance", and "monitoring". By adding "financial support" to its agenda, the IMF only laid down its new principal activity as creditor and credit intermediary for developing countries. The item of "technical assistance" went considerably further, because the IMF now claimed the right to have its say in the expansion of government capacities and the setting up of central banks. It thus enabled itself to ensure that key positions in economic ministries, as well as in central banks, were filled by people who were close to the IMF or at least shared its neoliberal views.

The most important amendment was that of "monitoring". The IMF's role had so far been limited to the enforcement of macroeconomic measures such as curbing the growth in money supply, fighting inflation, limiting budget deficits and reining in government debt. From now on, the IMF allowed itself to interfere in issues of "good governance", judicial reforms and the restructuring of the financial sector. In other words, by adopting the amendments the IMF formally paved its way for an even stronger encroachment on the sovereignty of debtor countries than before.

In 1979, the IMF officially presented its "structural adjustment programs" (SAP's) as a set of groundbreaking and universally applicable tools, subordinating the principle of conditionality to the increasing importance of global financial transactions, summed up under the headings "liberalization, deregulation, stabilization, and privatization". Although conditions were still individually tailored to each country requesting a loan, the basic features of the requirements were largely the same. They included, among others:

- Balancing the state budget through savings and expenditure cuts,

- Devaluating the national currency in order to enhance competitiveness,

- Restricting domestic lending by raising interest rates,

- Reducing import and foreign exchange controls,

- Orienting the economy towards just a few commercially attractive export goods,

- Removing restrictions on foreign investment,

- Privatizing state enterprises and state-owned assets,

- Providing legal guarantees for private entrepreneurship.

Each of these measures was nothing less than a slap in the face of the working people and the poor of the countries concerned. The wages of public employees were either frozen or reduced, and many of them lost their jobs. Spending cuts primarily targeted education and health care, thus affecting sectors that were and still are severely underfinanced in the developing world. Public schools were deprived of money, or school fees introduced in countries where illiteracy was and is among the biggest impediments to development. Medical services, already inadequate, were cut back even further. Subsidies for fuel were cancelled, forcing many households to live without power. The reduction or elimination of subsidies for basic foods spelled disaster for children who had already been suffering from malnutrition, and were now left to share the fate of many adults and die of starvation.

The devaluation of the national currency weakened the purchasing power of the working population that now had to pay higher prices for foreign products. Limiting domestic credit by rate hikes came as a blow to urban and rural small businesses. As they were dependent on cheap credit, thousands of small entrepreneurs went into bankruptcy, leaving their employees without jobs. The abolition of all import restrictions and the elimination of foreign exchange restrictions opened the gates for foreign capital. Products from all over the world now flowed freely into these countries, flooding the market with cheap goods. This influx had dramatic consequences, particularly in the agricultural sector. Small farmers were unable to compete with the prices of huge multinational food companies and were forced to declare bankruptcy. As a consequence, many African countries that had previously been exporters of food were transformed into food importers – and have remained so to this day.

The imposed focus on only a few commodities that were easy to market on a world scale led to a one-sided economic dependence of developing countries, causing a partial collapse of export earnings as soon as global market prices fell. Re-orientation of the agricultural economy towards products with a global demand such as coffee, tea and cotton, often led to a situation where the cultivation of century-old staple foods such as cassava, sweet potatoes and millet was neglected or discontinued.

The removal of restrictions on foreign investment drove many local businesses into bankruptcy, because they now had to compete with corporations that were financially, technically and logistically far superior to them. The privatization of state-owned businesses meant that basic service areas such as electricity and water or public transport were left to investors and speculators who, regardless of all social consequences, drove up prices dramatically after taking over the facilities.

In other words, the working population's standard of living was systematically lowered, problems of poverty, illiteracy and hunger were exacerbated, while social inequality was deepened and permanently consolidated. Major international banks, institutional investors and billionaire speculators, however, rubbed their hands with glee, because every single measure imposed by the IMF helped improve their investment and profit opportunities. In detail:

Cutbacks in state expenditure provided the countries with more money for servicing loans to foreign creditors. The devaluation of national currencies almost came as a gift from heaven for speculators: all they had to do was take out a loan in a foreign currency at the right time, show a little patience and then rake in a profit equaling the percentage of the devaluation.[12] Interest rate hikes aimed at reducing inflation fuelled currency speculation, which due to the rapid growth of the financial sector became more and more excessive, driving countries into even greater dependency on international financial markets and making governments increasingly compliant to the demands of foreign investors. Orienting countries' economies towards a few selected commodities increased their dependence and susceptibility to blackmail and created huge profits for multinational corporations which – due to the elimination of foreign investment restrictions – they were able to re-invest inside the countries, e.g. by buying up privatized state enterprises, thus raking in further gains.

No matter which individual measure of the IMF one considers, they all had three characteristics in common: They were harmful to the

---

[12]   If speculators from the dollar zone took out a loan in the currency of a developing country before a 50-% devaluation, they could pay it back afterwards and thus make a 50-% profit.

working population, they benefitted international investors and they pushed countries into even greater dependence on the global financial markets.

The fact that, despite this development, more and more countries turned to the IMF and applied for membership, is easily explained: Commercial banks only considered those countries creditworthy which submitted to the IMF's structural adjustment programs. If a developing country did not want to isolate itself, but wanted to continue participating in international economic and financial affairs, it was left with no other choice but to become a member of the IMF and accept its terms. This is why three quarters of all Latin American countries and two-thirds of all African countries had joined the IMF by the mid-1980s.

The Latin American Debt Crisis:
The IMF as Global Crisis Manager

The petrodollar glut of the sixties and seventies, combined with fren-
zied lending by international banks, raised the total amount of debt of
all developing countries by 600 %, increasing debt service (i.e. principal and interest payments) by 1,100 % between 1971 and 1982. The
total amount of claims against Latin America grew by 20.4 % annually
from 1975 to 1982. Foreign debt of all South American states, at $ 75
billion in 1975, amounted to more than $ 314 billion in 1983. Inter-
est rates of 15 % to 16 % drove the annual debt service, which had
stood at $12 billion in 1975, to $ 66 billion in 1982, an increase of
10 % per year. A crisis, the likes of which the world had not seen since
World War II, loomed on the horizon.

The first country facing trouble was Mexico. It depended on oil exports and had been hit hard by falling oil prices due to the global recession and the sudden increase in US interest rates. Foreign investors
withdrew $ 55 billion between 1979 and 1982, and the peso lost 67 %
of its value until February 1982, while the Mexican current account
deficit rose to $ 5.8 billion. When foreign banks refused to grant fur-
ther loans in the summer of 1982, the country faced bankruptcy.

Trading on the Mexican Stock Exchange was suspended. On August
12, 1982, a government delegation travelled to Washington, where
they informed the Chair of the Federal Reserve, the US Secretary of
the Treasury and the head of the IMF that Mexico could no longer
meet its payment obligations and therefore demanded a three-month

moratorium (suspension of payments). A quick inspection of the balance brought the sobering revelation that Mexico owed private banks all over the world more than $ 80 billion dollars. The representatives of Washington, Wall Street and the IMF knew immediately: A default of this magnitude could lead to bank failures in the US, Europe and Japan and cause a breakdown of the global financial system.

Within hours, IMF Managing Director Jacques de Larosière summoned the representatives of 800 banks to an emergency session in New York City. The only item on the agenda was the question of how a Mexican national bankruptcy could be averted. In order to gain at least a few weeks' time, the central banks of ten Western countries and the Basel *Bank for International Settlements* stepped into the breach with a bail-out. Then the IMF officially intervened, operating as a "mediator" between Mexico's government and private banks. Shortly afterwards, the IMF announced that it had wrested loans amounting to $ 5 billion from commercial banks in order to stabilize the Mexican economy and was itself willing to provide assistance payments amounting to $ 3.3 billion.

This was a rather euphemistic description of the following facts: In order to assure Mexico's ability to keep servicing its debt, its creditors were left with only one choice – providing it with even more loans. These, however, were not aimed at rescuing the country, but handed out solely for the benefit of creditor banks and tied to harsh conditions, required by the IMF, which significantly strengthened the power of precisely these banks and enabled them, among other things, to collect debt from Mexican companies more easily than before. The IMF itself provided a further $ 3.3 billion, but linked the provision of this sum to the rigorous enforcement of a comprehensive ten-point structural adjustment program, which led to a drastic reduction in real wages[13] and the abolition of state subsidies for staple foods. Along with per-

---

[13]   Real wages in Mexico dropped by 38 % between 1982 and 1986.

sistently high inflation, which in the next four years varied between 60 % and 90 % annually, the measures lowered the living standards of broad layers of the Mexican population and pushed a large section into abject poverty.

In December 1982, Brazil also declared a moratorium on the repayment of its international debt. Like the rest of South America, the country suffered from the fatal coincidence of US interest rate hikes, a sudden drop in exports due to the global recession, and rising inflation. Again, the IMF stepped in and forced the government to implement severe austerity measures against its people. Unscrupulously exploiting its counterpart's position of weakness, the IMF also demanded the abolition of import duties, by which the government had tried to protect its economy, primarily medium-sized Brazilian companies, from all-too-powerful international competition.

Despite all assertions to the contrary, the IMF did nothing to bring about a recovery of the Mexican or Brazilian economy, but rather profited from both countries' economic and financial plight in the most ruthless manner. Its sole objective was to ensure their future solvency and to use the crisis in order to improve conditions for investments and enhance income opportunities for foreign corporations and banks.

As the causes of the crisis were global in nature, it continued to spread. Until October 1983, 16 Latin American countries were forced to reschedule pre-existing debts. The largest four of them – Mexico, Brazil, Venezuela and Argentina – had alone accumulated debts of $ 176 billion to the private banking sector, $ 37 billion of which were owed to the largest eight US banks. Global debt of developing countries to commercial banks rose to $ 239 billion.

In each case, the IMF intervened as a globally operating financial fire brigade, imposing its structural adjustment programs on country after country. The implementation of the measures was discussed and decided at the Paris Club, which played an increasingly important role. Between 1956 and 1980 it had arranged agreements with debtor countries at an average rate of four agreements per year. From 1982 on, this number increased to more than ten per year, reaching its peak in 1989, when 24 agreements were reached.

It is worthwhile to take a closer look at this "club". It has no rules and no fixed written guidelines. Its members act according to five informally adopted "principles" – 'case-by-case treatment of debtor countries', 'consensus decision making', 'conditionality', 'solidarity' and 'comparability of treatment'.

'Case-by-case treatment' requires the club to tailor its actions to the particular situation of each debtor country. 'Consensus decision making' refers to the consent of all creditor countries, but not that of the debtor country. 'Conditionality' requires a debtor country to submit to an IMF program (stand-by program, Extended Fund Facility, Extended Credit Facility, Policy Support Instrument). The principle of 'solidarity' also exclusively refers to creditor countries, calling on them to act as a group and to take into consideration the claims of other creditor states when pushing through their own demands. Finally, 'comparable treatment' stipulates that a debtor country concluding an agreement with Paris Club creditors must not accept loans from third parties at less favorable conditions than those of the Paris Club.

Comparing the relationship between a debtor and a creditor to that between a defendant and a plaintiff, the Paris Club resembles a court in which the plaintiff simultaneously takes on the roles of prosecutor and judge, while the defendant is forced to waive his right to counsel. It is hardly surprising, then, that the meetings in the French Treasury, as a matter of principle, are held in secret. No lists of participants exist and no official records of the conferences are made. The only things preserved for posterity are the results of the meetings, which until 2012 have led to a total of 428 agreements with 90 countries taking out loans amounting to $ 573 billion.

The decisions of the Paris Club have led to a gigantic growth of global social inequality. While those living at the bottom of the social ladder are driven into even deeper poverty and permanently denied a decent existence, a tiny layer of ultra-rich have been given the opportunity of increasing their fortunes even in times of crisis. During the first years of the Latin American debt crisis, when a large part of the population was struggling hard for survival, international banks and their investors were able to rake in profits of $ 1.5 billion solely in Mexico and Brazil.

The fact that structural adjustment programs were bringing short-term advantages to the banks, while severely impairing long-term economic growth throughout South America and driving up debt due to low state revenues[14], could no longer be ignored after 1985 and spelled doom and gloom for international finance. In order to enable debtors to service their debt in the long run, this development had to be stopped by all means. But how?

In Washington, Ronald Reagan's Secretary of the Treasury, James A. Baker, together with the heads of the largest US banks and Paul A. Volcker, Chairman of the US Federal Reserve, forged a plan that Baker presented to the annual meeting of the IMF and the World Bank in the South Korean capital of Seoul in October 1985. The plan envisaged providing additional credit of $ 47 billion ($ 20 billion coming from private banks, $ 27 billion from the World Bank) over three years to fifteen countries, including ten in Latin America, which had accumulated a total debt of $ 437 billion. The states should thereby be enabled to create much-needed economic growth. However, the plan was not aimed at the world's poorest countries, but at countries that were defined as "middle-income". So it only covered states where an additional investment might pay off – as opposed to hopelessly impoverished states. Simultaneously, the IMF was to go on enforcing

---

[14] In Brazil, for example, public debt, which had stood at $ 70 billion in 1982, rose to $ 91 billion within two years.

its structural adjustment programs, while the World Bank was asked to play a bigger role than before in promoting the "modernization" of these economies.

The Baker Plan failed. Private banks shied away from risk because of South America's fragile situation. They only invested $ 12.8 billion between late 1985 and late 1988, while at the same time more than $ 30 billion dollars in interest flowed out of South America annually and capital flight continued in almost all countries because of economic instability. The situation did not improve for Western banks in the following years, and by the end of the 1980s, they were faced with a loss of several hundred million dollars. Everyone involved knew that new methods and a change in strategy were needed to cope with the huge mountain of problems that had accumulated over more than a decade.

A solution came into view after George Bush Sr. became President in 1989 and his Treasury Secretary Nicholas Brady took the matter into his own hands. Officially, Brady announced that the only way to counter the debt crisis was "to encourage the banks to voluntarily reduce their debt." In actual fact, his plan was nothing but an attempt to achieve the best possible deal for banks under the given circumstances, i.e. a combination of the lowest possible waiver and the highest possible yield for investors. Brady's strategy was based exclusively on the growth of the global financial sector and its investors' ever-increasing appetite for new profit opportunities.

In the case of Mexico, for example, the banks, at Brady's behest, were given the choice between two options: either to swap existing loans for 30-year 'debt reduction bonds' which meant a reduction of their total debt by 35 %, combined with higher interest rates, or to swap them for ordinary 30-year bonds without debt reduction at interest rates below normal market conditions. In order to enable them to make their interest payments at all, they were offered new loans covering 25 % of their total debt in 1989 at normal market rates.

This "offer of assistance" was subject to the condition that the interest and principal of these so-called "Brady Bonds" were collateralized by US Treasury bonds, which in turn could be traded in financial markets. What at first glance looked like a concession to developing countries actually amounted to a tightening of the screws, since the tradability of Brady bonds meant that the fate of developing countries no longer depended upon individual financial institutions, but was rather directly linked to international financial markets, and thus subjected to the cumulative power of Wall Street.

Soon, commercial banks bought up loans from developing countries, bundled them, and sold them to the banks of these countries, thus shifting their risks to them. Then they reinvested the money within these countries, a move that attracted currency speculators sensing profits, who took advantage of exchange rate fluctuations and thus inflicted considerable damage on the developing countries' economies. In other words, the IMF, whose representatives officially kept claiming to be promoting the "stabilization" of these economies, decisively and knowingly contributed to their destabilization.

Altogether, 566 stabilization and structural adjustment programs were implemented in 70 developing countries between 1980 and 1993. By May 1994, 18 countries had accepted Brady bonds worth $ 190 billion. The agreements had been reached primarily within the framework of the Paris Club, with the IMF always relying on the same partners: regional elites – small layers of extremely wealthy citizens, privileged by international capital – and corrupt governments acting in their interest. It is thus hardly surprising that the IMF occasionally showed its gratitude by turning a blind eye to the abolition of taxes on luxury goods for the rich, while at the same time supporting drastic tax increases for ordinary working people.

The Effects of "Structural Adjustment": Growing Resistance against the IMF

In pursuing its policies, the IMF depended not only on the support of national governments. It also needed the cooperation of the respective countries' repressive apparatuses, as the population's resistance against austerity measures grew with each tightening of conditions. After General Pinochet, in his own words, had "bathed the country in blood" during the years after his coup, mass protests erupted in Argentina when the government announced a 180-day wage freeze in order to reduce inflation and foreign debt in 1976. As in Chile, the military moved in, seized power and established a reign of terror, which over the following years cost the lives of 30,000 people, mainly trade unionists and students.

The situation in Africa and the rest of the world also deteriorated. In January 1977, almost all major cities in Egypt saw the outbreak of uprisings against the abolition of state subsidies for staple foods demanded by the IMF and the World Bank. 79 protesters were killed and more than 550 injured. In 1981, the Moroccan trade unions called for a general strike after the IMF had made a loan of $ 1.2 billion conditional upon the abolition of state subsidies on basic foods. In the course of the strike, thousands of young people rose up in the slums around Casablanca. The police moved in and killed more than 600 of them.

In 1984, trade unionists and young people in the Dominican Republic demonstrated against their government's austerity measures, which had been required by the IMF and had, among other things, led to a doubling of prices for medical products. 4,000 demonstrators were arrested, 50 died in a hail of police bullets. In 1989, several hundred demonstrators were killed in Venezuela after protesting against the abolition of subsidies for gasoline, an essential commodity especially for the poor.

In May 1986, about 20 students were killed at the Ahmadu Bello University in Zaria in Nigeria by security forces after protesting against the announcement of structural adjustment programs. More students were killed in similar protests at the Kaduna Polytechnic, the University of Benin, and the University of Lagos.

After the newly elected government of President Perez in Venezuela and the IMF agreed upon a structural adjustment program, which took effect on February 23, 1989, parts of the population rose up against the increase in the prices of petrol and public transport between February 28 and March 2. More than 600 people were killed and more than 1,000 injured.

In February 1990, students at the University of Niamey in Niger boycotted classes, protesting against cuts demanded by the IMF affecting the already inadequate education sector. During their peaceful demonstration, the police opened fire and, according to their own statements, killed three students.

From July 28 to August 2, 1990, a Muslim organization in Trinidad besieged government buildings in protest of austerity measures required by the IMF and held President Robinson and several cabinet members hostage. The conflict led to bloody clashes in Trinidad's capital, Port of Spain, which left at least 50 people dead.

Altogether, several thousand lives were lost in about 150 major protests against austerity measures required by governments and the IMF in 39 countries between 1976 and 1992. Despite this bloody record, the IMF never even contemplated reconsidering its destructive strategy. On the contrary, it persistently refused to deviate from its course, and in 1990 clearly indicated its future line of action by declaring its approval of the "Washington Consensus". This was the name given to a set of "basic principles" supported by political leaders in Washington, leading members of the US government, technocrats of the financial institutions, economic agencies of the US government, the US Federal Reserve, and Washington think tanks, which had been compiled by American economist and temporary IMF advisor John Williamson in 1989.

Williamson's ten principles did not represent a relaxation, but a tightening of the structural adjustment programs of 1979. In detail, the Washington Consensus called for budgetary discipline, a restructuring of priorities in public spending, tax reforms, liberalization of interest rates, a competitive exchange rate, liberalization of trade, the facilitation of foreign direct investment, privatization, deregulation and the protection of property rights.

Williamson himself displayed a biting sense of cynicism. The fact that high inflation hit the poor exceptionally hard, whereas the rich could avoid its effects by sending their money abroad, did not make him think about ways of preventing capital flight, but encouraged him to recommend austerity measures which further lowered the working people's general standard of living. He commented on the darker aspects of privatization by saying: "It can be a very corrupt process that enables a privileged elite to amass assets at a fraction of their value", only to add that it "just has to be done properly."

The timing of the Washington Consensus was no accident. While developing countries in Latin America, Africa and Asia were shaken to their foundations economically and socially, Europe, on the eve of the last decade of the twentieth century, was also facing a period of profound changes. Here, too, the IMF was about to play a decisive role in 'stabilizing economies' which meant nothing other than a further head-on assault on the living conditions of working people.

"Shock Therapy" for the Soviet Union:
The IMF and the Reintroduction of Capitalism

When Mikhail Gorbachev was appointed General Secretary of the Communist Party of the Soviet Union (CPSU) in March of 1985, the world's largest country was facing its deepest economic crisis ever. Central planning, which had been introduced after the revolution of 1917, had helped the once backward agricultural nation rise to global power, but from the early 1980s on, conditions had deteriorated continuously. The arms race with the United States had devoured vast sums of money during the "Cold War", and the war in Afghanistan had burdened public funds heavily after 1979. Mismanagement and corruption dominated the country. The economy, which had failed to keep up with the computer age and was no longer able to compete with the West internationally, was entering its sixth year of stagnation when Gorbachev took office.

Half a year after his inauguration, the situation worsened when Saudi Arabia announced the end of oil price fixing and the quadrupling of its oil output within the next six months. The resulting fall in prices led to a decline in revenues of $ 20 billion per year for the Soviet Union, thus causing an even greater shortage of foreign currency.

Gorbachev initially tried to shift the problems to the USSR's allies. He increased imports from the Eastern Bloc, forcing the Soviet Union's satellite states to accept Soviet oil at prices well above market value in exchange for their goods. Furthermore, he made ever greater concessions to capitalism. He paved the way for "joint ventures" (joint undertakings between Soviet state companies and Western corporations), allowed officials involved in the restructuring of public enterprises to withhold a share in profits, and tried to support the Soviet economy by means of extensive loans from abroad, thereby driving up national debt to a record $ 54 billion by the end of 1989.

When an application for an urgently needed jumbo loan to an international consortium of 300 banks was turned down, and even a rise in global oil prices following the Persian Gulf crisis did not help the Soviet Union back on its feet, Gorbachev desperately turned to the summit of the G7 (group of Seven = the seven leading industrialized nations from 1976 to 1998) in July 1990 to seek support from the US president. George Bush, however, had already developed his own plans in view of the decay of non-capitalist countries, which nobody could ignore any longer. As the G7 had mandated the European Union to concentrate their efforts on the former Eastern bloc countries, Bush called on the IMF and the World Bank to undertake a study of the Soviet economy.

IMF Managing Director Michel Camdessus, who had chaired the Paris Club from 1978 to 1984 and then worked as governor of the French Central Bank for three years, immediately sent a team of neoliberal economists to Moscow to monitor the situation and gather as much information as possible from officials at all major Soviet financial institutions. After five months of research, on December 19, 1990, the group published a paper which did not leave a shred of doubt about the path which Bush and the IMF had in mind for the Soviet Union: A radical transformation into a capitalist country by means of a shock program based on the Chilean model.

Section 2 of the paper presented by Camdessus stated: "Ideally, a path of gradual reform could be laid out which would minimize economic disturbance and lead to an early harvesting of the fruits of increased economic efficiency. But we know of no such path ..." Section 7 stated: "The initial phase will involve significant distortions and a transition to market prices will affect those with low incomes..."

While the US Government and IMF leadership began preparations for the transition, the economic situation of the Soviet Union continued to deteriorate. Financial problems and a lack of investment caused oil exports to decline by more than 50 % from 125 million tons to 60 million tons in March 1991. Simultaneously, the political situation escalated. In January 1991, three months after he had been awarded the Nobel Peace Prize, Gorbachev brutally suppressed an independence movement in the Baltic States[15]. In March and April 1991, coal miners in Siberia went on several strikes that led to the loss of more than two million working days. To make matters worse for Gorbachev, Boris Yeltsin, one of his sharpest political adversaries, became increasingly powerful. The longtime party boss of Sverdlovsk, who had resigned from the CPSU in 1990, openly pursued a right-wing, market-oriented course. On April 9, 1991, Yeltsin's steady rise prompted Gorbachev go on the offensive and present an "anti-crisis program" that promised "a fully market-oriented pricing system", the decentralization of foreign trade, and the privatization of "loss-making" companies.

By deciding to end the socialization of enterprises, to abolish the state monopoly on foreign trade, and to reintroduce private ownership of the means of production, Gorbachev not only sealed the fate of the Soviet Union. He also deprived the "nomenklatura" – the ruling layer of party bureaucrats that he himself belonged to – of their social basis, as their privileges were inextricably tied to the bureaucratic structures of central planning. Gorbachev thus paved the way for a new propertied class, which would find its most ardent pioneer in his adversary Boris Yeltsin, and go down in history as the caste of "oligarchs".

---

[15] On January 13, 1991, also called "Bloody Sunday in Vilnius", Soviet tanks caused a blood bath among peaceful demonstrators demanding their country's independence from the Soviet Union that left 14 people dead and more than a thousand injured in Lithuania's capital.

While politicians and scientists around the world hailed the "final victory of market economy over socialism", some going as far as proclaiming the "end of history" (US sociologist Francis Fukuyama), the IMF took an unusually cautious stance. While it had always been impatient in imposing loans on developing countries and bringing them into economic dependence as quickly as possible, it displayed remarkable restraint towards the developments in the former Soviet Union. There were two good reasons for the IMF's hesitance: Firstly, the former Soviet Union still had no functioning state institutions that could guarantee the protection of private property, and secondly, it was not yet clear how much resistance the working people would put up against the announced reforms.

On August 19, 1991, Moscow became the scene of a coup by conservative hardliners against Gorbachev. Although it was put down after three days and ended with Gorbachev's return to office, it clearly showed the General Secretary's weakness and his lack of support among the population. The beneficiary was Boris Yeltsin, whose power rapidly grew and who was now subjected to a special kind of aptitude test by the IMF: After several Soviet officials had expressed negative feelings about the shock program, details of which were now out in the open, the Fund used its annual meeting in Bangkok to declare that it insisted upon the total repayment of Soviet debt, and that it expected the Soviet republics to provide the necessary means by eliminating all subsidies for industry and agriculture and slashing the defense budget. Yeltsin got the message and responded by replacing Premier Silayev with Yegor Gaidar, a former business editor of the "Pravda" who had abandoned his commitment to central planning and turned into an ardent neoliberal admirer of Milton Friedman and his "Chicago Boys".

Gaidar immediately carried out the IMF's instructions, thus accelerating the economic disintegration of the Soviet Union. By the end of the year, industrial production had fallen by 8 % and gross domestic product had decreased by 17 %. Only 3 of 237 state-funded construction projects planned for that year reached completion. Imports from the satellite states slumped by 63 %, exports to these countries by 57 %. Imports from capitalist countries fell by 32 %.

A catastrophic harvest and the rationing of food in November and December 1991 finally sealed Gorbachev's fate. The last General Secretary of the CPSU resigned from office on December 25, 1991. On December 31, 1991, the Soviet Union formally ceased to exist and on January 2, 1992, the IMF had finally achieved its goal: Led by Boris Yeltsin and Yegor Gaidar, Russia officially entered the era of economic "shock therapy".

The IMF sent Augusto Lopez-Claros to Moscow as its resident representative. Lopez-Claros was a neo-liberal economist who had worked as a professor of economics at the University of Chile in Santiago during the Pinochet dictatorship from 1982 to 1984 and had later served as the head of a research team for the Chilean ministry of health, gaining a wealth of experience in passing on the effects of economic crises to working people. His way of carrying out a "transition from totalitarianism to democracy" – the title of a lecture held by Lopez-Claros in 1994 – plunged Russia into a state of social devastation the likes of which the country had not even experienced during the Soviet Union's worst times in both world wars.

Within the first year of shock therapy, the prices of basic foods – which had until then been state-subsidized – skyrocketed. The price of eggs increased by 1,900 %, that of bread by 4,300 % and that of milk by 4,800 %. Over the next four years, Russian GDP fell by an average of 42 %, industrial production fell by 46 % and agricultural production fell by 32 %. Due to the IMF's reluctance to lend[16], the Russian government ordered its own Central Bank to resort to the printing press. This in turn fueled hyperinflation to a level of over 1,000 %, wiped out

---

[16] In July 1992, the IMF approved a $ 1 billion stand-by loan that was to be available as of 1993. It was followed by two "system transformation loans" of $ 1.5 billion each in 1993 and 1994.

the savings of working people and pushed an ever greater number of them below the poverty line.

54 The disparity between the increase in the prices of agricultural machinery, fertilizers and pesticides between 1991 and 1994 by a factor of more than 520 and the increase in the prices of agricultural products by a factor of 90 led to a rural exodus, resulting in the depopulation of 17,000 settlements between 1991 and 2003.

The simultaneous radical opening of domestic markets to foreign goods opened up tremendous sales opportunities for Western corporations and, due to the lack of competitiveness of domestic production, led to the demise of hundreds of thousands of small and medium-sized businesses. The privatization of large state-owned corporations provided a tiny layer of former party and state officials with the opportunity of enriching themselves in two ways: Firstly, by closing down non-competitive enterprises and selling off their assets, and secondly by taking over a huge portion of former state enterprises, especially in the areas of energy, telecommunications and non-ferrous metals, thus creating the foundations for immense fortunes.

According to estimates by the New York Times, ex-officials-turned-oligarchs from 1993 to 1998 deprived the Russian economy of $ 200 billion to $ 500 billion by transferring the money out of the country. Even top US government officials spoke of a "plunder" of the Soviet Union. While Russia's national debt grew and the country became increasingly dependent on international financial institutions such as the IMF and the Paris and London Clubs, international financial capital was rejoicing, because the money went directly to the accounts of Western banks, enabling them to rake in huge profits.

It was the weakest members of society – old people, children, the poor and the handicapped – that were hit hardest by the transformation of a planned economy to a market-oriented system. Pensions were often not paid for months on end, while – formerly free-of-charge – medical services could not be maintained because of the ruthless commercial-ization of health care. Prices for medicines soared to such levels that even average urban wage earners could no longer afford medication. Between 1991 and 1994, the number of fatalities due to tuberculosis increased by 87 %. Between 1989 and 1995, life expectancy for men dropped from 63.3 to 58.4 years and that of women from 74.4 to 72.1 years.

During the same period, the birth rate declined by 30 %. The total population of Russia decreased by almost 10 million to 142 million within 12 years. Alcoholism, mental illnesses, crime and homeless-ness spread like wildfire. Social rights and services such as childcare and child benefits, which had been available to everyone in the Soviet Union, were dismantled. Many parents were no longer able to care for their children. Teenagers were forced to prostitute themselves, and an increasing number of "street kids" were seen in metropolitan ar-eas – phenomena that had been unknown during the Soviet era even in the worst times of war.

The promises that had been made to the people of the former Soviet Union when the shock program was first implemented seem almost like a macabre joke in retrospect. In 1992, the IMF had predicted that after a brief period of minor limitations, the introduction of capitalism would lead to unprecedented prosperity. In actual fact, the impover-ishment of the working population and the rise of a layer of extremely wealthy nouveau riche favored by international capital led to a level of social inequality which the country had not known even in the dark-est times of tsarism. A particularly disgusting form of cynicism was displayed by the international media, which continued to justify the country's social and economic decline as a necessary phase that would pave the way for the "democratization" and the "liberalization" of a hitherto totalitarian state.

The IMF's and the United States' real attitude towards the develop-ment of democracy in the former Soviet Union became apparent in

1993, when Boris Yeltsin, after a short period of dual power, tried to impose a new constitution. After parliament had rejected his draft constitution and removed him as president, Yeltsin called in military tanks and ordered them to open fire on the parliamentary buildings. The ensuing battle ended in a massacre in which, according to government figures, 187 people lost their lives and 437 were injured. None of this prompted the G 7 to withhold loans of $ 43.3 billion, which it had agreed to before the blood bath. The act of murder did not bother the IMF, either. Its system transformation loan of $ 3 billion even helped consolidate the position of a president who had not shied away from defying the constitution and securing dictatorial powers with brute force.

There was worse to come. In 1994, Yeltsin started a war against Chechnya, which claimed eighty thousand lives within the following two years. Even air raids against the civilian population or the siege of the Chechnyan capital of Grozny, during which 25,000 people were killed in January 1994, did not keep the IMF from handing out further loans of $ 1.5 billion, $ 6.4 billion and $ 18.9 billion in 1994, 1995 and 1996. And as if that wasn't enough, the IMF even used mounting domestic opposition against Yeltsin and his war politics for the purpose of linking disbursement of the loans to a further liberalization of trade, an increase in taxes and sharp cuts in the pension system of the country.

Despite all assertions to the contrary, the IMF (as well as Western governments) never intended to "democratize" Russia or help the Russian people to greater prosperity and more freedom. The exclusive objective of the IMF's policy was to break down all barriers for international finance capital and provide it with the opportunity of seizing the country's wealth, of exploiting cheap labor and creating ideal conditions for global financial institutions to rake in millions and billions by means of currency speculation, lending and short-term investments.

The result is well-known. The re-introduction of capitalism led to legendary fortunes for a tiny layer of ultra-rich profiteers and a life of opulent luxury for a minority of upstarts. For the vast majority of the population, however, it brought lower life expectancy, inadequate medical care, poor educational opportunities, living conditions at or below the poverty line and, above all, the destruction of their dreams and hopes for a better future.

Christine Lagarde, 2007

Post-Apartheid South Africa:
The IMF and the ANC Join Forces against the People

"Nelson Mandela was a courageous and visionary leader... The extraordinary global reach of Nelson Mandela's admirers is testimony to his profound contribution to making South Africa and the world a better place."

These words in commemoration of Nelson Mandela, spoken in December 2013, did not come from one of his comrades, but from the IMF's managing director Christine Lagarde, and truly surprised many listeners. Had not the racist apartheid regime been among the founding members of the IMF? Had Mandela not been convicted and sentenced to life imprisonment as its avowed enemy?

They had. Both the pro-racist attitude of the IMF as well as Mandela's decade-long confinement as a political prisoner are well-established facts. But there is a historical link between the two that explains Christine Lagarde's downright enthusiastic tone. However, this link has been hushed up to this day by the official media, and for good reason: Firstly, it would deprive one of the most glorified heroes of our time of his halo and secondly, it would reveal the true motives behind the worshipping of Mandela by arch-conservative politicians and business leaders such as Christine Lagarde. In addition, it would also provide an explanation for why South Africa, more than 25 years after the end of racial segregation, is further away from the ideal of a just society than ever before. To better understand this, let us take a quick look at the country's history:

Since the beginning of the twentieth century, the South African system of racial segregation, called Apartheid, enabled a wealthy white minority to lead a life as colonial masters, while keeping the black majority of the population in a state of modern slavery. When South Africa experienced a huge economic boom in the 1960s, it was solely the ruling white minority that benefitted from it. The ensuing massive increase in social inequality led to the first major protests by the black majority. Growing popular resistance was boosted by the success of the liberation movements in the rest of Africa and the emergence of the Black Power movement in the United States.

In the 1970s, uprisings and bloody clashes became more frequent. The brutality of the racist regime manifested itself in 1976 when a police unit confronted protesting students in the black township of Soweto, near Johannesburg, and opened fire. Hundreds of children and teenagers were killed in the streets, and numerous others tortured after their arrest in what the police later called an "attempt to determine the ringleaders".

The global outrage over the massacre did not prevent the IMF from continuing to support the South African government, granting it loans of more than $ 2 billion in the following years. But neither these funds nor regular loans granted by the World Bank could prevent popular resistance from growing and increasingly destabilizing the regime's reign.

In order to safeguard its own interests and to keep South Africa dependent on American good will even under a possible new regime, the US government decided in 1983 to radically change its course. Under the pretext of devoting itself to the fight for racial equality, Washington prohibited all further payments to the regime in Pretoria. At the same time, it applied a new tactic behind the scenes and urged the South African government to start secret negotiations with potential future rulers of the country.

At that time, the representatives of the *Confederation of South African Trade Unions* (COSATU) and the *African National Congress* (ANC) under the leadership of Nelson Mandela, which had been banned since 1960, were seen as the most likely new rulers. Mandela had been arrested in 1961 and sentenced to life imprisonment in 1964. He served most of his term in the now-famous prison on Robben Island.

In order to avert the impending end of their own rule, in 1985, the South African government began to organize several high-level secret meetings. In Zambia, a group of South African industrialists under the leadership of Gavin Reilly, chairman of the *Anglo-American Mining Company*, met with exiled leaders of the ANC. In Great Britain, Thabo Mbeki, number two in the ranks of the ANC behind Mandela, met leading business leaders in the villa of *Consolidated Gold Fields*, a corporation that could look back on more than a hundred years of experience in profiting from racism by exploiting black mine workers.

The most important meetings, however, took place in a suburb of Cape Town. Shielded from the public eye, intelligence chief Neil Barnard and President Pieter Botha got together with Nelson Mandela in Pollsmoor prison. During these meetings Botha, also known as "the crocodile" for his extremely tough stance on race issues, made Mandela an offer: If Mandela were prepared to encourage the ANC to commit itself to renouncing violence against the old regime and abandon its demand for a state-run economy and the partial collectivization of monopolistic enterprises, banks and natural resources – as laid down in the ANC's Freedom Charter – and above all to recognize all foreign debt of the apartheid regime, then the South African government would, for its part, consider lifting the ban on the ANC and think about releasing Mandela from prison.[17]

Although the number of supporters of the ANC was rapidly increasing at that time, and the racist regime was just as rapidly losing ground, its collapse only being a matter of time, Mandela and his leading comrades-in-arms accepted the offer behind the backs of their followers. Botha's successor De Klerk released Mandela from prison on February 2, 1990.

Twenty years later De Klerk said that releasing Mandela from prison had prevented "a disaster". Intelligence chief Neil Barnard clarified what kind of disaster De Klerk meant in a later interview when he said, "At that time we had to prepare for dealing with a prolonged revolution."

In fact, South Africa's social development at the end of the 1980's clearly pointed to a revolutionary overthrow of the racist regime. An ever-increasing part of the population demanded the expulsion of the rich white upper class, a fair distribution of land among poor peasants, the expropriation of the much-hated banks and corporations, and legal prosecution of the crimes of the racist regime. The fact that not a single one of these objectives was achieved is mainly due to Mandela's and his fellow ANC leaders' cooperation with the South African government and the business community of the country.

Nelson Mandela's historical achievement was not – as is officially claimed – to have abolished racial segregation. The end of apartheid would have been sealed in 1990 anyway, even without his help. Mandela's outstanding role was in fact to prevent the expropriation of the ruling class and the expulsion of foreign investors at a decisive moment in history, thus subordinating the interests of the black majority

---

[17] Details of the meetings are contained in several interviews that intelligence chief Barnard gave in later years.

of the population to the interests of the old ruling clique and its allies in the international financial communities. This is precisely the reason for today's ongoing praise in the global media and by some of the most conservative representatives of business and politics, including the Managing Director of the IMF.

Mandela was richly rewarded for his cooperation by a true campaign of deification in the international media, aligning him with Abraham Lincoln, George Washington and Martin Luther King, and by receiving the Nobel Peace Prize in 1993 (which he voluntarily shared with the racist De Klerk). Mandela for his part returned the favor by signing a secret Memorandum of Understanding to the IMF together with other ANC leaders before the 1994 elections and declaring that in case of a takeover of power, they would guarantee market principles, implement drastic budget cuts, set high interest rates, and enable international capital to gain free access to all areas of the South African economy.

During the "transitional period" from 1990 to 1994, Mandela and his comrades already bent over backwards to prove their reliability to the old regime, the IMF and the World Bank. First they renamed the ANC's "Department of Economic Planning" the "Department of Economic Policy", and made a politically moderate professor of economics its chairman. Then they agreed on a division of labor between the ANC, the trade unions and the government, which was first applied in September 1991. When the government, in complete agreement with the IMF, announced the introduction of a 10 % value added tax, a wave of indignation among the black population swept the country. ANC and COSATU immediately placed themselves at the top of the protest movement of 3.5 million people, organized a two-day general strike to let off steam, then waited a few weeks without doing anything and finally approved the new tax.

This was not to remain the only case of deception with particularly harmful consequences for the poorest sections of the black population.

The ANC's "Reconstruction and Development Program", which also served as a platform for the elections in May 1994, promised the reallocation of 30 % of large-scale land holdings. In agreement with the World Bank and the IMF, the ANC later dropped the demands and replaced them by a "market-oriented land reform", which comprised less than 1 % of all land holdings.

Five months before the elections in April 1994, a transitional executive committee took control of the South African parliament. Instead of finally chasing the racist National Party out of office after 45 years of brutal oppression, the ANC accepted their representatives as partners and jointly accepted an $ 850 million loan from the IMF, which was officially declared a relief measure to alleviate the population's plight after a drought.

However, since this drought period had already ended 18 months earlier, and its consequences had long since been overcome, many skeptics wondered about the true background of the loan. They were right in doing so: according to an article in South Africa's daily newspaper *Business Day* in March 1994, the loan was tied to explosive and pioneering secret arrangements. They called not only for the elimination of import tariffs and a reduction in government spending and wage cuts in the public sector, but also for the designation of two veteran representatives of the racist regime to the posts of minister of finance and governor of the Central Bank, which were of utmost importance to international finance.

A month later, the ANC honored its secret agreement with the IMF. Although winning the elections by an overwhelming majority of 62.5 %, the IMF not only accepted the Zulu nationalist party, but also the racist National Party into a "government of national unity" and appointed their representatives to the posts demanded for them by the IMF.

In public, the leaders of the ANC justified their cooperative behavior towards the old regime by claiming to be promoting a policy of "reconciliation" and "peaceful settlement". However, during the following years it became increasingly apparent that this strategy primarily benefitted the old regime, international capital and particularly the leadership of the ANC. The working population, however, soon had to learn what Nelson Mandela meant when, at the opening of Parliament in 1995, he said, "We must free ourselves from the culture of entitlement mentality."

The policies pursued by Mandela during his presidency until 1999, along with his finance minister and the Central Bank governor in cooperation with the IMF, had nothing whatsoever to do with the promises that Mandela and the ANC had given before the election. On the contrary: They were a slap in the face of the working people and the poor, but came as a godsend to the old elite of the country as well as to international banks and corporations.

Thousands of jobs were eliminated and salaries reduced in the public sector, while corporations and the wealthy were granted tax relief[18]. The state pension fund was 'restructured' for the benefit of those who for decades had stood in the service of the old racist regime. Large corporations were permitted to transfer huge sums abroad and relocate their headquarters out of the country, which, together with the abolition of import duties, led to the loss of thousands of jobs inside the country. The Central Bank was allowed to raise the interest rate by double-digit amounts, much to the delight of foreign currency speculators and to the detriment of small domestic businesses that were driven into bankruptcy. A law against usury that provided for an interest rate ceiling of 32 % on loans was abolished.

---

[18] The corporate tax was successively lowered from 48 % in 1994 to 30 % in 1999.

The stock market soared. Pension funds generated surpluses and, contrary to all previous regulations, were put exclusively under the control of employers by the government. Arms deliveries, even to dictatorships, were not suspended, but extended. The financial system was deregulated to such an extent that investments constantly declined, and more and more capital went into international speculation. Finance, insurance and real estate became the most profitable sectors of the economy, while industrial production shrank.

The ANC's promise to the majority of the black population that temporary deterioration would lead to long-term improvements in their living standards, turned out to be a downright lie. Both under Mandela, as well as under his successors Mbeki and Zuma, material conditions for the less wealthy constantly worsened. Instead of an annual employment growth of 3 % to 4 %, which the government had promised, 1 % to 4 % of jobs were lost each year during the second half of the 1990s. Total unemployment among blacks rose from 36 % in 1994 to 47 % in 2004. The average income among the black population fell by 19 % in real terms, while that of whites increased by 15 %. A survey in 1996 showed that nearly one and a half million black South African households were located in slums. In 2011, the number had grown to almost two million, an increase of about 30 %.

The deterioration of the education and health care systems particularly disadvantaged the lower social layers. More and more schools introduced school fees, so that even the poorest were forced to pay for school uniforms, books, writing materials and transport to school. A government survey in 2001 showed that the public school system in South Africa was in a disastrous state. While billions were earned on the stock market and through financial speculation, 27 % of all schools had no running water, 43 % had no electricity, and 80 % had neither a library nor any computers.

The health sector was in even worse shape. Due to cutbacks in the state budget and the privatization of medical services, diseases such as tuberculosis, cholera, malaria and AIDS spread faster and wider than during the apartheid era. Due to the poor state of the water supply and price increases imposed by European companies after the privatization of many water systems, several ten thousand children died each year from diarrheal diseases. One of the most horrible indicators of the social devastation brought about during the first ten years of the ANC's rule was the average reduction of life expectancy by twelve years from 65 to 52 years.

Not only the social divide between rich whites and poor blacks, but also social inequality within the black population increased steadily. To improve its image, in 2004, the government adopted the *Black Economic Empowerment Program*. It instructed authorities to fill positions in the administration and in large industrial firms with more black applicants than before. One of the consequences was that the proportion of black managers in listed companies increased from 0 % to 20 %. For the lower income groups, however, the measure remained completely meaningless.

More important, however, were the politics of the black trade union leaders. They developed exceptional skills in buffering protests against the deterioration of living standards and diffusing the energies of striking workers, thereby helping the country's leaders to stick to their neoliberal course. In return, the government richly rewarded them for their cooperation. Mandela's companion Cyril Ramaphosa, a founding member of the *Mine Workers' Union* and the COSATU, is a perfect example of this layer. Born into a poor family in the township of Soweto, he has meanwhile turned into a tycoon, a billionaire several times over, and is counted among the richest people of South Africa. (Mandela himself also died a wealthy man, leaving his heirs stakes in more than two hundred companies.)

The implementation of policies demanded by the IMF and enforced by the ANC has turned South Africa into a country where the gap between those who live in abundance and those who languish in poverty is greater than almost anywhere else in the world. Reality has reduced to absurdity the main argument of "peaceful co-existence and non-violence", advanced time and again by Nelson Mandela and the ANC to justify their willingness to compromise with the old regime. Today's South Africa has one of the highest crime rates in the world and is considered to be one of the most unsafe and most dangerous countries in the world.

The only people who can feel safe in South Africa these days are the top 10 % of the population who claim nearly 50 % of national household income and lead a life of luxury – in sealed residential areas behind high walls, surrounded by barbed wire, alarm systems, and guarded by heavily-armed security services. It was probably this kind of life that Christine Lagarde referred to when she said that Nelson Mandela had made South Africa "a better place".

Yugoslavia and the IMF:
Setting the Stage for War in Europe

A particularly dark chapter of the IMF's history in relation to Europe was written in the former Socialist Republic of Yugoslavia. In the 1980s and 1990s, the IMF contributed significantly to the impoverishment of a people of 24 million, helped break up a multi-ethnic state and thereby created the conditions for the bloodiest conflicts on European soil since World War II.

Yugoslavia had come into existence by the merger of the six republics of Slovenia, Croatia, Bosnia-Herzegovina, Montenegro, Serbia, Macedonia and the Serbian autonomous provinces of Kosovo and Vojvodina in 1945. It had broken off relations with the Soviet Union and turned away from the Eastern Bloc in 1948. Because of the nationalization of its key industries and its banking sector, it did not belong to the capitalist West either, so its leadership under President Tito embarked on what he called a "third path" between capitalism and socialism. From an objective point of view, Tito's political strategy was nothing more than a set of cleverly designed maneuvers, intended to exploit Cold War tensions between Western powers and the Soviet Union for the benefit of the ruling clique of Yugoslav party officials.

Because of its strategically advantageous location on the edge of the oil-rich Middle East, Yugoslavia played an important role as a front and buffer state for the US's strategy of "containment" of Soviet influence. It was for precisely this reason that Yugoslavia was given membership in the IMF and granted generous loans by American banks.

During the post-war boom, the Yugoslav economy therefore experienced a major economic upswing. Increasing imports of consumer goods, investment in health and education, and the doubling of exports of manufactured goods between 1954 and 1960 led to a substantial improvement of living conditions, but at the same time increased Yugoslavia's dependence upon foreign capital. In addition, rapid economic growth favored the industrialized North over the backward and largely commodity-dependent South, creating an imbalance that was to have disastrous consequences.

The petrodollar glut of the 1970s led to an increase in the scope of loans. From 1966 to 1979, industrial production grew by an average of 7.1 % per year. However, since Yugoslav industrial and agricultural products were only partially competitive in Western markets, too little foreign currency flowed back into the country to reduce the increasing amount of debt. Foreign debt, which had stood at just over $ 2 billion in 1970, rose to $ 18 billion in 1980, equaling more than a quarter of the national income.

The US policy of high interest rates at the end of the 1970s abruptly inflated the cost of repaying loans and, along with rising inflation, contributed to the increasing distress of international creditors. At the beginning of the 1980s, many of the more than 600 Western banks exposed to Yugoslavia demanded their money back or refused to grant new loans. The IMF stepped in with a standby loan, and in return demanded an increase in exports, inflation control, and a reduction in government spending. Enforcement of the measures, however, dragged on, and time was pressing as the situation rapidly deteriorated.

When a short time later the country was faced with the threat of default, Belgrade's US Ambassador Lawrence Eagleburger encouraged Western industrialized nations, commercial banks and the IMF to join forces and form an alliance that later became known as the "Friends of Yugoslavia". It organized a first rescheduling of debt in 1983 and tied a $ 600 million loan from the IMF – the largest loan ever granted to an applicant state until that date – to the condition that the government – and thus the tax-paying working people of Yugoslavia – not only take liability for public debt amounting to $ 5.5 billion, but also for private debt amounting to $ 10.9 billion. In addition, Yugoslav companies were obliged to settle their foreign debts irrespective of their financial situation, which meant that in many cases banks received their money, while workers were no longer paid.

71

Both measures were taken in close consultation with the US Treasury and the representatives of Wall Street, and obviously fell in line with a US National Security Agency policy directive stating that greater efforts were required "to overthrow Communist governments and parties" – which, for the United States, included non-aligned Yugoslavia – "in a quiet revolution."

The measures proved to be highly effective. Businesses collapsed by the dozen, unemployment soared, and average wages fell by 40 % until 1985. The officially proclaimed goal of the IMF, supposedly to reduce the debt ratio, was never achieved. Instead, Yugoslavia, which paid $ 30 billion in interest, compound interest and principal until 1988, became the most highly indebted country in Europe during the second half of the 1980s and, according to the World Bank, ranked seventh among the group of "Highly Indebted Countries" behind Brazil, Mexico, Argentina, Nigeria, the Philippines and Venezuela. The daily hardship of ordinary people led to tensions between the constituent republics that were affected to varying degrees[19] by the social decline. Trying to exploit the situation, right-wing politicians began to strike nationalist and separatist tones.

Three further debt-rescheduling arrangements, the "enhanced surveillance" of the country by the IMF, and a loan of $ 300 million granted under the fourth rescheduling arrangement, did not improve the situ-

---

[19] Unemployment in Slovenia in the 1980s never exceeded the 5 % mark, while it rose to almost 60 % in Kosovo.

ation, but only benefitted the creditors. Economic growth dropped to 2.4 % in 1987 and fell to zero in 1988. Capital kept flowing out of the country, and unemployment continued to rise. While 45 % of foreign revenue went into debt service, the country experienced its first food shortages. People started to get angry. Economic decline accelerated, and in 1987, the government was once again faced with the threat of default. A wave of labor disputes rocked the country, reaching its peak in 1987 / 88 with over 4,000 strikes and demonstrations.

Irrespective of all popular resistance against the dictates of the banks, the IMF did not hesitate to exploit the changing tide in world politics to take an even tougher stance towards Yugoslavia. Due to the dawning collapse of the Soviet Union and its satellite states, ruling Yugoslav officials began to look for ways of retaining their privileges despite the threatening breakdown of the old structures. After a brief period of disorientation, they embarked upon the same path that the party-and-state-officials-turned-oligarchs of the Soviet Union were pursuing: They shook off their past as proponents of economic planning, actively helped destroy the old structures of self-government, and started promoting privatization in order to gradually take possession of former public property for themselves. Prime Minister Ante Markovic provided an exceptionally illustrative example for this sort of political transformation. Having begun his career as an ardent partisan in the struggle against fascism, he ended up a fervent supporter of neoliberalism and a wealthy entrepreneur in Austria.

Joining forces with the IMF, the old and the new rulers of Yugoslavia now drove the country into final bankruptcy. Starting in 1988, foreign capital, which until then had only been accepted as investment in joint ventures, was given carte blanche for investments in industry, banking, insurance and the service sector. Since assets were classified according to their 'carrying value', which in comparison to capitalist countries was far too low, Western investors were heading for a veritable bonanza. While they were busy filling their pockets, 250 enterprises went bankrupt or were liquidated, and 89,400 employees lost their jobs in

1989. Almost 900 firms followed until September 1990, with more than half a million people being laid off. Serbia, Bosnia-Herzegovina, Macedonia and Kosovo were hit hardest by the wave of closures.

On the orders of the IMF, wages were frozen at their November 1989 level. By the end of the year inflation reached 70 %, then increased to 140 % in 1991, to 937 % in 1992, and reached 1,134 % in 1993. Living conditions for the majority of the population declined to the level of a developing nation, primarily affecting the poorer parts of the country such as Kosovo, Macedonia and Montenegro. At the same time, anger grew in the more affluent provinces such as Serbia, Croatia and Slovenia, because the central government forced their governments to pay a greater share than financially weaker regions. In 1989, Serbia introduced taxes on Slovenian and Croatian products. In return Croatia began to collect special charges on Serbian holiday homes on the Adriatic Sea. Slovenia followed suit by suspending its payments to the Development Fund for Kosovo, Macedonia and Montenegro, thus depriving the region of 40 % of all payments.

Nationalist rhetoric spread, and nationalist ideas gained a growing number of followers. The first calls for the independence of individual provinces could be heard, and alerted major Western powers. While in the past, the US had often felt the need to pay dearly for Yugoslavia's complaisance because of its zigzag course between the major powers, the foreseeable fall of the Soviet regime now opened up completely new perspectives. The region could not only be completely subordinated to the world market economically, but also fragmented and turned into a strategic geopolitical ally by applying the principle of "divide and conquer". The calls for the establishment of independent states led the US to jump on the bandwagon and support these trends. Germany, which had become a political and economic powerhouse within the EU after its re-unification in 1989, and urgently needed the Balkans as a sales and investment market, took the same stand. With the help of Austria, Germany supported Croatia's and Slovenia's independence movements financially and by means of its intelligence service.

To finally seal the disintegration of old Yugoslavia, the IMF and the World Bank once again applied the thumbscrews in the fall of 1989. The implementation of their common "Financial Operations Act" led to the complete deregulation of trade. The Yugoslav market was flooded with foreign goods, many of them subsidized by the European Community. Domestic industrial production plunged by more than 10 %. The central government was prohibited from taking out loans from its own Central Bank. It was also forced to make spending cuts to the amount of 5 % of gross domestic product, which it did at the expense of social benefits.

A new 'corporate law' introduced to promote the privatization of companies provided a so-called 'exit mechanism', according to which businesses that had been insolvent for 30 days had to come to terms with their creditors. As the government was prohibited from intervening and the National Bank was banned from granting further loans to the companies concerned, the law enabled creditor banks to convert their share of the loans into shares in the company's assets. To prevent exactly this from happening, a majority of state-owned enterprises in the first half of 1990 halted all wage payments, whereupon half a million workers – one in five – remained unpaid for months.

The most far-reaching measure, however, was the suspension of payments to the provinces and the constituent republics. On the orders of the IMF, the money was no longer available for distribution within the country, but had to be used to pay off debts to the Paris and London Clubs. This provocative interruption of financial flows between the capital Belgrade and the provinces led to a disastrous response which, however, definitely suited the major powers' strategy of fragmentation: Slovenia and Croatia reacted by stopping their payments to the Compensation Fund and began to publicly speculate about applying for membership in the European Community.

After the IMF had thus laid the economic groundwork for the final breakup of Yugoslavia, governments led by the US and Germany now suddenly insisted on individual ethnic groups' right to self-determination – a demand which until then had never played even a marginal role in their politics. At the same time they promoted and supported separatists materially, and unleashed a veritable media battle in order to incite racial hatred among 26 ethnic groups that had been living together peacefully for almost half a century, with 30 % of marriages being contracted between different ethnic groups. Such a strategy proved successful: in 1990, nationalist parties prevailed in the elections held in the constituent republics. This was soon followed by the first incidents of violence between different ethnic groups.

75

The support of the separatists by the major powers increased tensions with Serbia, which declared itself the successor state to Yugoslavia and insisted on the old territorial unity. The situation was exacerbated when in early 1991, the Serbian government of Slobodan Milošević ordered about $ 1.8 billion to be printed by the National Bank in order to pay outstanding government wages, thus undermining the IMF program. The United Nations responded by imposing an embargo that was drastically tightened the following year.

In June 1991, Croatia and Slovenia declared their independence. That same month, the Yugoslav People's Army intervened. The so-called Ten-Day War against Slovenia ensued, which quickly shifted to Croatia and led to a war that expanded into Bosnia in 1992 and lasted until 1995. When Croatia announced its own constitution and declared itself a sovereign state on December 22, 1991, Germany responded quickly and recognized its independence just one day later, in complete disregard of the conditions required by the European Community, such as the protection of minorities. The European Community as a whole did not take its own rules too seriously, either, and followed suit on January 15, 1992. The United Nations recognized Croatia's independence in May 1992.

The IMF responded to the new situation by freezing Yugoslavia's membership, accepting Slovenia and Croatia as new members, and allocating Yugoslavia's outstanding debt to international creditors to them in December 1992. Thus, Croatia had to take on 28.5 % of the total debt of former Yugoslavia, while Slovenia had to shoulder 16.4 %. The lion's share of 36.5 % of all Yugoslav debt was imposed upon Serbia and Montenegro. Despite the hostilities, which lasted until 1995, the IMF subsequently negotiated new loans with Croatia, Slovenia and Macedonia, which, however, were not intended for reconstruction or the elimination of war damages, but for debt service. A document signed by the Croatian government under Franjo Tudjman in 1993 led to even more plant closings, pushed wages partly below the poverty line and drove unemployment up to 19.1 % in 1994 – all for the benefit of international creditors.

The working population of Bosnia-Herzegovina did not fare any better. After NATO fighter jets had flown 52,000 combat missions between April 1993 and March 1995 and more than 33,000 civilians and almost as many soldiers had been killed, the US and the EU imposed a new "market-oriented" constitution upon the country in their Dayton Agreement. In addition, the country was militarily subordinated to NATO and politically subordinated to Swedish Prime Minister Carl Bildt as "high representative" for reconstruction – the hitherto deepest intrusion into the sovereignty of a European country after World War II.

Economic policy formulation for Bosnia and Herzegovina was placed in the hands of the IMF, the World Bank, and the *European Bank for Reconstruction and Development*. The constitution, brought about without a Constituent Assembly, provided that the Director of the Central Bank be appointed by the IMF and "not be a citizen of Bosnia and Herzegovina or a neighboring state." The Central Bank itself was prohibited from printing new money or introducing its own currency for a period of six years. International loans were to be used exclusively for the repayment of debts to international creditors and for funding the deployment of military as defined in the Dayton Agreement, but were not to be used for the financing of economic reconstruction. Thus a bridge loan in the amount of $ 37 million granted by the Dutch government was not used to relieve the suffering of war victims, but to repay the Dutch Central Bank, which had lent the money to the IMF to enable it to pay off outstanding debt.

77

The opening of former Yugoslavia's successor states to international capital and their subordination to the common regime of the UN, NATO and the EU, reminiscent of colonial times, was still not enough to satisfy Western powers. Notwithstanding the large number of war victims and the traumatization of large parts of the population, they began looking for further ways to completely subjugate the country. When nationalist forces began to emerge in Kosovo and other parts of former Yugoslavia, Germany, the UK and the US jumped at the opportunity, sent in their intelligence, and contributed decisively to the fact that protests which started out peacefully were turned into bloody civil-war-like clashes.

The conflicts were carefully nurtured until Serbian leader Milošević forcibly intervened, thus providing the major powers with the desired pretext for a more aggressive approach. Western powers ordered him to the negotiating table in Rambouillet, France, and demanded his signature under a contract which, among other things, provided for the deployment of 50,000 NATO troops authorized to give instruction to the police and the country's authorities, and also entitled to using airports, ports, railway stations and roads free of charge at any time.

After Milošević reacted as expected and rejected the contract, the armed forces of NATO and the United States – for the first time without a mandate from the UN or the *Organization for Security and Cooperation in Europe* (OSCE) – unleashed the largest military action on European soil since World War II. Under the pretext of putting an end to human rights violations in order to avoid a humanitarian catastrophe, fifteen cities were subjected to aerial bombings around the clock for 78 days. Cluster bombs and uranium ammunition were used, vital water supply systems and heating plants were destroyed, and 344 schools and 33 hospitals were razed to the ground.

78   After the fighting ended, the alliance installed a paramilitary government that maintained close ties to organized crime. While more than half the world's heroin trade passed through the country in the coming years, the IMF and the German *Commerzbank* took complete control of the banking system. Whenever squeezing billions out of a completely impoverished population turned out to be too difficult, they were now able to resort to freshly laundered money for repaying the loans of international investors for reconstruction.

Germany's first active participation in a war since the founding of the *Bundeswehr* in 1956, made possible by the Social Democrat – Green coalition government of Chancellor Schröder and vice-chancellor Fischer almost a decade after reunification, marked the country's return to the circle of major powers. The US, on the other hand, primarily pursued the main objective of demonstrating its military strength by excessively applying its latest weapons technology. The goal was to enhance the United States' claim to dominance within NATO[20] by sending send clear messages to Russia, which had emerged from the dissolution of the Soviet Union, and to China, whose economy was rapidly expanding, as well as to the increasingly powerful European Union[21] that was rapidly gaining economic and military strength.

The end of the Kosovo war in a way closed a circle for the IMF. Its neoliberal policies, enforced by granting loans tied to crippling condi-

---

[20] Target reconnaissance, target selection, and target planning, as well as in-flight refueling and the use of precision-guided ammunition throughout the war, were exclusively controlled by the US Army.

[21] At the EU summit in Cologne, for example, a "restructuring of the European defense industry" had been discussed and joint consultations of foreign and defense ministers had been proposed in order to improve the effectiveness of command and communication structures for military operations in cases of emergency.

tions, had led to the destabilization of an entire region. A country that had once known economic growth, full employment, free health care, free education, maternity leave, six weeks' annual leave, low rents and affordable food, a literacy rate of over 90 % and a life expectancy of 72 years, had been completely destroyed and its population thrown back to the status of a developing country. The IMF's programs had prepared the ground on which Western intelligence and the national media, also financed by the West, had been able to launch a massive campaign which prompted people, driven by unemployment and desperation, to commit ethnic crimes, finally leading to the seizure of power by right-wing nationalists. Without the IMF's systematic groundwork, the humanitarian catastrophe of the 1990s in the Balkans would not have been possible.

Protest in Seoul (South Korea) against neoliberal structural change,
which first began with the IMF's measures in response to the Asian Crisis, October 13, 2008.

The IMF and the Asian Crisis:
A Demonstration of Power

As a result of the increasing globalization of financial markets, Asian economies which, starting in the 1960s, had recorded the world's highest growth rates, offered increasingly interesting opportunities to international investors. At the beginning of the 1990s, the IMF and the US Treasury urged the states in the region to facilitate access to their markets for foreign capital. The governments immediately carried out liberalization measures that drove the overall level of foreign bank loans in Indonesia, South Korea, Malaysia, Thailand and the Philippines to a record total of more than $ 260 billion by the end of 1996.

However, 50 % to 67 % of these were short-term loans that did not go into the real economy but were used as "hot money" for the purchase of stocks and real estate, areas in which fast and high profits could be made. Asian banks immediately capitalized on the resulting price increases, especially in real estate, by using them for the securitization of loans. This led into a dangerous spiral, a fact which did not bother foreign investors such as US pension funds and Wall Street banks, because on the one hand they made splendid profits due to high interest rates for risky assets, and on the other hand, the risk no longer lay with them but with the Asian banks.

The IMF did not feel obliged to warn against the looming dangers, either. Instead, it kept supporting the trend even when disaster started to unfold. "Private capital flows have gained greatest importance for the international monetary system, and an increasingly open and liberal system has proven to be advantageous to the world economy." The IMF made this statement on September 21, 1997 – at a time when US billionaire George Soros and other speculators were already betting against the Thai Baht currency and the starting signal for a devastating cross-border chain reaction had already been given.

Shortly afterwards, events were set in motion at breakneck speed. The real estate bubble burst, the baht had to be devalued several times, foreign investors withdrew large amounts of capital. Uncertainty among donors spread to other countries, resulting in an outflow of capital on an unprecedented scale.[22] Within a few weeks a large part of the Asian banking system lay in tatters. Since no private foreign capital was available, the governments of the countries affected had no choice but to turn to the IMF as a lender of last resort.

The following events unfolded exactly according to a script written by the IMF. Credit-seeking countries declared their readiness to make concessions in a "letter of intent" – pre-arranged with the representatives of the Fund – to make the public believe that the measures were not being required by the IMF, but had been "suggested" by the country's official authorities and then "accepted" by the IMF.

Thailand took the lead in December 1997. The country asked for a loan, and in return agreed to principally prioritize foreign debt, lay off 30,000 state employees, close 56 insolvent financial institutions and reduce government spending. Indonesia followed and announced a budget restructuring, the closure of 16 banks and a rise in interest rates on foreign capital of up to 80 % in order to lure investors back into the country.

---

[22] After an inflow of $ 92.8 billion in 1996, Indonesia, South Korea, Malaysia, Thailand, and the Philippines recorded a net outflow of $ 12.1 billion in 1997.

None of these measures helped to stabilize the faltering economies. On the contrary, all of them worsened the situation, directly leading to recession, and thus transforming the financial crisis into a severe and profound economic crisis. Large parts of the population that had already lost more than half their purchasing power by the currency devaluation now had to struggle for sheer survival. 83

The representatives of international finance capital, however, could not only breathe a sigh of relief, but start rolling up their sleeves in preparation for further action, since the intervention of the IMF not only secured the repayment of their loans, but also provided them with completely new profit opportunities. The closure of financial institutions and the consequent collapse of companies, combined with a further liberalization of the capital market, meant that wealthy foreign investors could purchase the strategically most important industries at rock-bottom prices. Hedge funds and major US banks did not miss out on this opportunity – thus plunging the economies affected into even greater dependency on international financial markets.

The way in which the IMF favored global funders, overrode national law, and passed all the consequences of the crisis on to working people could best be seen in the case of South Korea which, besides Thailand and Indonesia, was hit hardest by the crisis. In contrast to all other countries in which the IMF until then had implemented its structural adjustment programs, South Korea was not an emerging market but a highly developed industrial country, and therefore a competitor to the United States, particularly in the fields of cars and electronics.

South Korea had undergone breathtaking development. The country had risen from an isolated agrarian state to the eleventh-largest economy in the world in just under four decades. In the years before the crisis, the growth rate had stood at 7 %, and the unemployment rate had remained below 3 %. With inflation running at about 5 %, exchange rates were stable and a surplus was expected in the state budget. The overall picture was only tarnished in one respect: Due to the liberal-

84

ization of the financial sector, required especially by the IMF and the US, the Korean government had increasingly facilitated raising foreign capital for domestic banks and credit institutions since the beginning of the 1990s. In this way, South Korea's mountain of debt had grown from $ 44 billion in 1993 to $ 120 billion in September 1997.

The dangers generated by this dependence were well known. In September 1997, the Japanese government had proposed introducing an "Asian Monetary Fund" at a meeting of Asian finance ministers, because it was worried about Japanese banks that were deeply involved in the lending business with Korea, with $ 25 billion of outstanding debt in their books. The Fund was to be provided with $ 100 billion which were to be contributed by Japan, China, Taiwan, Hong Kong, Singapore and subjected to less severe conditions than the funds granted by the IMF. Due to the violent rejection by the US Treasury, which saw the interests of American banks adversely affected by such agreements, the plan was dropped.

Barely two months after the Japanese proposal, the Asian crisis spread to South Korea. The stock market in Seoul collapsed, and international currency speculators began to bet against the South Korean currency, the won. The Bank of Korea tried to defend the won, but its foreign exchange reserves turned out to be insufficient. Foreign investors panicked and withdrew their capital to such an extent that the government was left with no other choice but to turn to the IMF for help and apply for a loan in the amount of $ 20 billion.

A team of economists headed by Hubert Neiss, the Austrian director of the IMF for Asia, rushed to Seoul and undertook a hasty appraisal of the situation. It turned out that $ 20 billion would not be nearly enough as South Korea's foreign exchange reserves had already dropped below the $ 6 billion mark and short-term external debt stood at $ 100 billion, more than twice the amount expected. A total of 11 major US banks, 10 Japanese financial institutions and 80 European banks were imminently threatened by their Korean debtors' default.

IMF Managing Director Camdessus immediately travelled to Seoul to take part in the negotiations himself. On December 2, 1997, the South Korean government closed nine major banks in consultation with the IMF, promising their creditors comprehensive compensation. Only 24 hours later, the government came up with the required "Policy Framework Document" which was "accepted" by the IMF a day later. On December 5, 1997, the IMF and South Korea agreed on the largest stand-by credit hitherto granted by the IMF. Its total volume amounted to $ 58.4 billion, with $ 21.2 billion coming from the IMF itself, $ 14.2 billion from the World Bank and the *Asian Development Bank*, and $ 23.1 billion being provided by the governments of the United States, Japan and the European Union.

In return for the loan, the South Korean government had to implement a three-year structural adjustment program that was linked to more than one hundred conditions, its disbursement being "phased" sevenfold, i.e. subjected to seven inspections by the lender. The day after the agreement was concluded, investors seemed pleased. The South Korean stock index's daily gain reached an all-time high of 7 %. But just two days later, the tide turned abruptly. Capital outflows increased to $ 1 billion a day, the won collapsed and within the next two weeks lost 39 % of its value. South Korea was heading for bankruptcy.

Three incidents, although completely unrelated to each other, had triggered the turnaround. First, on December 8, the South Korean government had announced that it would nationalize two banks rather than close them as required by the IMF. Second, the conglomerate Daewoo had publicly announced that it wanted to buy SsangYong Motors, which was drowning in debt, and impose a portion of its debt on the banks involved, in defiance of the demands of the IMF. Third, the three candidates for the upcoming presidential election on December 18 had reacted to the population's violent rejection of the IMF by publicly distancing themselves from the deal between the government and the IMF, thus calling future cooperation with the Fund into question. Although this was done solely for electoral reasons, international investors regarded the combination of these three factors as undue insubordination, and answered accordingly.

86   The IMF responded by setting an example and showing the world what to expect of countries that did not fully submit to its dictates in times of crisis. During the two weeks leading up to Christmas it tightened its demands drastically and enforced their implementation in even less time. Kim Dae-jung, who was elected as the new President on December 18, and who had already pledged his future support to IMF Managing Director Camdessus behind the back of his constituents in a confidential letter, got the message, ostentatiously went before the public and declared that he would open up the Korean market to foreign capital and restore international investors' lost confidence.

While acknowledging the gesture of submission with satisfaction, the IMF did not remain inactive until Kim took office in January, but concluded a new agreement with South Korea on December 24. It was unequalled in its relentlessness and intransigence. On December 5, the IMF had required that all foreign investors be allowed to purchase 50 % of authorized Korean firms as of December 30, 1997 and 55 % as of the end of 1998. Now it insisted on a written assurance by the government that foreign investors be allowed to acquire 55 % of authorized Korean companies' capital as of December 30 1997 and 100 % as of the end of 1998. The stock market, of which only 26 % had been open to foreigners, was completely opened for foreign capital.

The Central Bank was prohibited from giving loans to tumbling South Korean companies or banks. Foreign banks and financial institutions, on the other hand, were allowed to invest in domestic financial institutions without limitations as of March 1998. The interest rate ceiling of 40 % was lifted, and South Korean banks that had run into payment difficulties were made more attractive to investors by transferring their bad loans onto the bailout fund *Korea Asset Management Cooperation*, thus imposing their debt on the tax-paying population. Completely disempowered in matters of fiscal and monetary policy, the Ministry of Finance was threatened with the suspension of payment of individual loan tranches (a measure that would have directly led to another wave of currency speculation) if it did not follow all instructions.

South Korea's economy also had to undergo a drastic restructuring. Trade barriers were removed; foreign imports – especially from Japan – were facilitated. In contrast, borrowing was significantly impeded for the giant South Korean family corporations, and they were advised to enter into "strategic alliances" with foreign companies. At the same time the rights of fund companies and shareholders were massively expanded in the interest of investors – two crucial steps towards the further subjugation of South Korean corporations under foreign capital. The labor market was "reformed" and made "more flexible", i.e. work requirements were tightened, working hours extended, layoffs facilitated, severance pay and vacation days cancelled and temporary work permits made possible. The resistance of Korean workers, who initially fiercely opposed these interventions, was forcefully put down. The corrupt trade union bureaucracy proved to be particularly helpful in this regard, entering a "triple alliance" with the government and employers' organizations and back-stabbing their rank-and-file members to such an extent that IMF Managing Director Camdessus, in an article for the *Korea Times*, thanked them for their "high sense of responsibility towards the government and the business community".

The Christmas agreement between the IMF and the South Korean government led to economic and social shocks, the likes of which the country had never before experienced. 14 of the 30 largest South Korean business conglomerates collapsed in the first half of 1998, several thousand medium-sized businesses had to be shut down. Mass layoffs, a hitherto unknown phenomenon in Korea, drove the unemployment rate to 6.8 % by the end of 1998. Acquisitions, closures and mergers reduced the number of commercial banks from 33 to 22, and that of trade banks from 30 to 9. Gross domestic product fell by 5.7 %; housing prices fell by 12.4 %. National debt, which had stood at 6 % in 1996, tripled, resulting in higher interest and principal payments by public authorities, which in turn led to tax increases and reductions of social benefits.

88   Starting in mid-1998, foreign companies and banks swept the country like locusts. Large corporations such as *General Motors, Ford, Renault, Royal Dutch / Shell* and BASF, major banks such as *Goldman Sachs* and the *Deutsche Bank* or US investment companies such as *Newbridge Capital* and *Lone Star* not only secured themselves corporate investments or acquisitions at bargain prices,[23] but also promptly benefitted from the new "flexible" labor laws. The working population, on the other hand, fell into a bottomless abyss. Up to eight thousand workers per day were laid off, the number of irregular temporary workers and day laborers increased to 52 %. The abbreviation IMF was used as a synonym for "I am fired" and "IMF orphans" became a household word for children whose parents were no longer able to feed them and therefore had to hand them over to state orphanages.

The real income of urban households fell by 20 % within a year, and at the end of 1998 reached its lowest level in 35 years. The deregulation of the credit card business demanded by the IMF led one and a half million South Koreans to indebt themselves and slip into personal bankruptcy by the end of 1998, almost four times as many as in 1997. Unemployment benefits were limited to a few higher-paid workers of large companies, and were totally inadequate from a social point of view. In 1999, only 15.5 % of all laid-off workers received financial support from the state. As a result, beggars and homeless people flooded the streets. The number of poor people as well as the suicide rate rose sharply.

---

[23]   To give an example of the price erosion of South Korean enterprises: The market value of *Samsung Electronics* dropped from $ 6.75 billion in October 1997 to $ 2.4 billion within six months.

During the first half of 1998, property crimes increased by 60 %, compared to the same period in 1997. The number of prison inmates rose by 20 % within six months.

Things looked quite different at the other end of the social ladder. While foreign investors were able to record high profits, the salaries of the top ten percent of senior executives increased by 10 %, and the assets of the richest 20 % of society increased by 13 %. Private schools sprang up all over, sales of luxury goods boomed, and the gap between the rich and the poor deepened in a country that had for decades prided itself on its social equality.

The fact that the South Korean economy began to grow again in 1999 did not signal a return to the situation before the crisis for working people. Deregulation of the labor market, increased tax burdens, limited benefits and high rates of inflation rigidified social relations and led to a permanent reduction of living standards. Above all, the IMF's measures did not eliminate the structural problems of South Korea, but rather exacerbated them. The country's dependence on the world market, in particular its dependence on China and the United States in the area of memory chips and information technology, was significantly increased, and the government's ability to intervene in future crises was reduced, while its subjugation to US and international finance capital was ensured at least for the medium term.

Wage Caps and Higher Prices:
The IMF's Policy of "Poverty Reduction"

Until the 1970s, the IMF was given very little attention by the majority of the population of industrialized countries. In the 1980s, it was only occasionally taken note of by the public, such as during the extensive media coverage of the protests against the IMF World Bank meeting in West Berlin in 1988. All this changed radically in the 1990s. On the one hand, the IMF's intervention in Russia and the Eastern Bloc had moved its sphere of influence geographically closer to Europe. On the other hand, a growing number of NGOs took an increasingly critical stand against the detrimental effects of its policies. In particular, many young people were outraged because the world's poorest countries were forced to settle debts with multi-billion dollar financial institutions in industrialized countries instead of being allowed to use the money at home in order to combat hunger, disease and illiteracy.

In 1994, fifty years after the Bretton Woods conference, about five hundred NGOs globally joined forces and started a campaign directed against the IMF and the World Bank, claiming that "Fifty years is enough." At the same time, the first preparations were made for the "Jubilee 2000 Movement", which called for full debt cancellation for the world's poorest countries at the turn of the millennium, winning hundreds of thousands of followers in forty countries during the following years.

In 1996, the IMF and the World Bank surprised the international public by stepping forward and announcing to the world a shift in their strategy towards their poorest debtors. After having addressed the debt problems of mainly middle-income countries in the 1980s, they announced they would now turn their attention to the world's poorest countries. The "Heavily Indebted Poor Countries (HIPC) Initiative" would allow these countries to escape from the debt trap by achieving sustainable debt levels, thus paving the way into a less dismal future, especially for countries in sub-Saharan Africa.

Some of the organizations campaigning for a haircut or for complete debt cancellation attributed the IMF's alleged policy change to the pressure which their international activities had exerted on the financial organizations, and welcomed their "rethinking". Others responded more skeptically and, as it soon turned out, were proven right. The HIPC Initiative was by no means a new strategy, but merely a modified and economically updated version of the *Enhanced Structural Adjustment Facility* (ESAF), created by the IMF in 1987. Under ESAF, poor countries in financial distress had been granted loans of up to 140 % and in exceptional cases of up to 185 % of their quota with the IMF under a three-year SAP program at an interest rate of 0.5 %, semi-annual repayment starting after 5 ½ years, with a maturity of ten years. Under the ESAF arrangement a total of $ 10.1 billion had been granted which, however, had almost exclusively been used to pay off old debts, and which had not reduced, but rather increased the indebtedness of the countries concerned. Despite their favorable terms, the loans had only temporarily eased the countries' problems while worsening them considerably in the long term.

In the meantime, the situation of the poorest countries had also deteriorated due to the changing structure of their debt. In the initial phase of their indebtedness, their creditors had predominantly been commercial banks. Since then, their creditors had become mostly either states or international financial institutions. Since these were far more powerful and able to exert much greater pressure than individual banks, poor countries were now negotiating from an even weaker position.

A comparison of access provisions and implementation rules of HIPC and ESAF provides evidence of this change. The only countries eligible for the HIPC initiative were those that fulfilled the following criteria: Their annual per capita income had to be below the $ 925 determined by the *International Development Association* of the World Bank as a reference value for the poverty of countries, their foreign debt had to exceed 150 % of their annual export earnings or 250 % of annual state revenue, and they had to have undergone an IMF structural adjustment program and fulfilled its conditions to the satisfaction of the Fund. In 1996, only half the countries that had qualified for ESAF nine years earlier fulfilled these criteria.

The World Bank itself described the desolate state of these countries in one of its documents in these words: "Of the six hundred million people in HIPC countries, more than half live in absolute poverty, i.e. on less than one dollar per day. Average life expectancy is thirteen years below that of industrial states and seven years below that of other low-income countries. More children than in other developing countries die at birth or before their fifth birthday and even fewer will go to school."

The strategists of the IMF and the World Bank had apparently, after a careful examination of their impoverished clients, come to the conclusion that a total of 39 countries – that was the number of countries considered eligible for the HIPC Initiative – would not be able to service their debt in the long term due to their disastrous social conditions. In order to avoid a complete default, those countries that showed willingness to cooperate with the IMF were to be granted financial alleviation until "debt sustainability" was restored, i.e. until they were able to once again service their old debt including interest, compound interest, principal, surcharges on overdue payments and rescheduling fines, all to be paid on the basis of previous conditions. Neither the IMF nor the World Bank ever intended to rid the poorest countries of their debt. Their sole aim was to prevent them from collapsing financially in order to be able to cash in on them again later. To meet this objective, the IMF even provided a clear definition of "debt sustainability": in order to reach this status, a country's debt burden had to fall below one and a half times the value of its export earnings.

The annual "Human Development Index" of the United Nations of 1999 indicated that the income ratio between the richest and the poorest 20 % of the population of the wealthiest countries in the world, which had stood at 30 : 1 in 1960, had risen to 74 : 1 in 1997, and that half the world's population, then comprising three billion people, had to live on less than $ 2 a day, while the total assets of the richest three billionaires in the world exceeded the entire possessions of 600 million people in the least developed countries.

The provisions of the HIPC Initiative did not contain the slightest indication that this trend would change in favor of the poor from now on. Not surprisingly, the protests all over the world did not subside. On the contrary, they spread, grew in ferocity, expanded to the US, and assumed a dynamism that truly worried political leaders and their organizations. In June 1999, the EU and the G8 summits in Cologne, Germany, witnessed the largest protests since the anti-IMF campaign of 1988. Responding to the pressure of the streets and fearing even larger protests, the G8 requested that the IMF and the World Bank "revise" their HIPC initiative. Just three months later, both organizations responded by presenting their new enhanced HIPC II Initiative, called "Poverty Reduction and Growth Facility" (PRGS), to the public.

The presentation was accompanied by the carefully staged admission that both organizations had so far shown a lack of transparency and had "patronized" the world's poorest countries. As if repenting for its sins of the past, the IMF announced that it wanted to give up its current practice of imposing unilaterally devised measures on these states without prior consultation. Instead it would, within the framework of its new strategy, introduce so-called "Poverty Reduction Strategy Papers" (PRSP), which would be worked out by the governments of the countries concerned in cooperation with political parties, parliament, the trade unions, church organizations, NGOs, cooperatives, and interest groups, and which would include concepts for "good governance" and a strategy for poverty reduction. In this way, the IMF would promote 'participation' and 'ownership' while the governments, on the basis of adopting the strategy paper, could expect debt service relief (the partial elimination of interest and compound interest payment) and, following the actual implementation of the paper, partial debt relief.

At first glance this seemed like sincere rethinking and no less than a change in policy by the international financial organizations. At second glance, however, it turned out to be nothing more than another act of deceiving the public, cleverly thought out by the strategists of the IMF and the World Bank. By requesting that the governments of the poorest states develop a strategy for combating poverty in cooperation with domestic organizations, the IMF and the World Bank created the impression that the core of the problem was purely national, its focus lying between the government and the people, and that the international financial organizations were trying to help solve this problem from the outside. In actual fact, it was the hemorrhaging of these countries by exactly these financial institutions that, above all, had furthered and solidified poverty and prevented a successful fight against it in recent years.

While almost all international media led the global public to believe that the international financial organizations, inspired by humanitarian considerations, had changed their course, virtually nothing was changed in reality. Just as the earlier structural adjustment programs, the strategy papers for poverty reduction were still subject to a harsh form of conditionality. For example, the measures designed to reduce poverty were embedded in a catalog of exactly those measures which since the 1970s had led to the spread of poverty and hunger, the surge in debt, and growing dependency of the countries concerned upon international donors.

Such a "new" practice of having the poverty reduction strategy papers reviewed, and then either accepted or rejected by the IMF after completion by the respective governments, was nothing but window dressing. Most poor countries had gathered sufficient experience with the IMF for decades, so that their mostly corrupt governments were easily able to supply the Fund with strategy papers tailored exactly to its needs and quickly finding its approval. Rather than setting in motion a democratic process or promoting "ownership", the IMF thus enforced an even closer cooperation with the governments of poor countries.

A quick glance at the amount of debt that was actually forgiven shows that debt relief primarily applied to unattended debt, and that its cancellation was nothing but a normal write-off on money that creditors could no longer expect to be repaid anyway. In any case, debt service by the countries concerned decreased at a much lower rate than their debt level. The German organization *erlassjahr.de* calculated that after reaching the decision point, debt service for 29 countries fell from $ 3.7 billion to $ 2.7 billion during the first year, then increased to $ 3 billion and for the next five years remained at this level. According to the organization, this was due to the fact that the countries, besides servicing old debt, had to take out new loans that were usually granted at customary conditions.

Besides, the commitments to partial debt relief under HIPC, as well as under HIPC II, only applied to multilateral creditors, i.e. the international financial organizations. Bilateral creditors, i.e. states and commercial banks, were encouraged to also waive a large part of their debt, but in most cases refused to comply. Thus, in August 2006, 54 countries that had pledged their proportional debt relief under HIPC and waived claims of $ 2 billion stood in contrast to 46 countries with claims amounting to $ 1.8 billion that had insisted on their demands.

Commercial creditors reacted even more harshly. More than 90 % insisted on their demands, some of them with vigor. Until August 2006,

44 of them took their claims to court, including, for example, the German company *Klöckner Humboldt Deutz*, which, supported by the German government, sued the Democratic Republic of Congo for the repayment of outstanding liabilities amounting to 70 million euros. Although the IMF distanced itself from the behavior of commercial creditors, it showed its true face on the issue when its executive board rejected the proposal to set up a legal aid fund for HIPCs that were taken to court because of their cancellation of old debt.

Once again it was the working people and the poor who turned out to be the victims of this development. Although the past had clearly shown the detrimental impact of the liberalization of trade and the agricultural sector, the deregulation of the financial sector, flexible labor markets and the privatization of public utilities, the IMF and governments, even within the framework of "poverty reduction", mercilessly insisted upon the implementation of these measures. This unbending position, among other things, led to the absurdity that the strategy papers for poverty reduction in the countries of Gambia, Ghana, Guinea, Malawi, Mali, Mozambique, Nicaragua, Sierra Leone and Yemen demanded an expansion of privatization of the water supply and along with it an increase in water prices, while calling for "a reduction of labor costs by lowering the minimum wage" in Burkina Faso.

While the first HIPC Initiative had required the countries concerned to first undergo a three-year IMF program to reach the "decision point" and after three more years arrive at the "completion point", HIPC II left the duration of the "interim period" open. As it turned out, in some countries this phase lasted for up to 15 years, during which the IMF not only largely determined their economic policies, but also monitored implementation of the measures it had demanded, and ordered sanctions in case individual arrangements were disregarded.

Although the protests against the IMF did not subside and even reached new heights at its annual meeting in Prague in 2000, which was broken off early because of violent riots, the IMF did not change its course for the time being. However, in June 2005, it took the world by surprise. On the basis of a proposal made by the G8 finance ministers, it announced the introduction of the "Multilateral Debt Relief Initiative" (MDRI) as a supplement to HIPC and HIPC II. According to the IMF, it was to provide a "complete debt relief" for some countries. The international media immediately took up the issue. Many spoke of the long-awaited "breakthrough" and a "fundamental change of policy", while some NGOs in turn hastened to attribute the announcement of debt relief to their own efforts. However, just as in the past, it was worth looking behind the facade, as once again there was a wide discrepancy between the IMF's publicly disseminated humanitarian slogans and the harsh reality.

Compared to ESAF, HIPC, and HIPC II, the number of countries eligible for MDRI was once again reduced. Only two categories of countries could be considered – firstly those that had reached their completion point under the HIPC II Initiative and thus had aligned their macro-economic policies and their public finances according to the requirements of the IMF for years (some for more than a decade), and secondly those whose per-capita income lay below $ 380 a year. In addition, "full" debt relief was granted exclusively by the IMF, the International Development Association of the World Bank (IDA) and the African Development Fund (AfDF). Contrary to the HIPC initiatives, no other creditors were invited to participate in the debt relief scheme this time. Also, the scheme primarily involved long-standing debt, while new loans, taken out before adoption of MDRI, were not taken into account. Also, forgiven debt was to be offset against future loans.

So the only cases in which the IMF renounced its demands were actually not those in which there was no prospect of debt repayment, but those in which the respective country, by implementing all reforms demanded by the IMF, had created the necessary preconditions for international finance capital to not only compensate for its losses, but to operate without restrictions and accumulate new profits in the future.

Since the IMF was accurately informed about the finances of its poorest borrowing countries and the default of these countries had been foreseeable for years, there is only one explanation for its conduct: high-risk lending was never meant to help these countries rebuild their economies and their infrastructure or eradicate poverty and hunger, but rather was aimed at luring them into a debt trap from the outset in order to exploit their foreseeable hardship by extorting concessions which they would never have consented to under normal conditions.

The Argentine Crisis and the IMF:
Enforcing the largest State Bankruptcy ever

Argentina, which had been one of the richest countries in the world until the 1930s, went through various phases of stagnation and instability in the 1950s and 1960s. After a succession of several military regimes, a coup in 1976 established the reign of terror under Jorge Videla. In order to implement an economic program of neoliberal reforms against the will of the majority of the population, his junta unleashed the so-called "Dirty War", which lasted from 1976 to 1978 and in which 30,000 political dissidents 'disappeared'. The continuation of this policy of neoliberalism after the end of Videla's dictatorship and its drastic intensification under conditions of parliamentary democracy was mainly due to the fact that the country had known a constant and reliable factor in its economic and financial policy since the 1950s – the International Monetary Fund.

Regardless of all forms of rule and despite all human rights violations, the IMF concluded 19 agreements with various Argentine governments from 1956 to 1999, and in return for the arrangement of loans exerted considerable influence on the country's economic and social development. To attract foreign capital, Videla promoted the liberalization of trade, the deregulation of the financial system, and the privatization of a number of state-owned enterprises. Following the Chilean model, he also reduced wages, imposed a government ban on strikes, increased interest rates to attract international investors, and eliminated all trade barriers to facilitate imports of foreign goods.

Multinational corporations, Western banks, and speculators did not hesitate to avail themselves of the new opportunities, closely cooperating with the Argentine army leadership. When Videla's rule ended in 1983 due to growing public opposition, many generals had become entrepreneurs and millionaires.[24] The share of wages in GDP, however, had fallen from 43 % to 22 % within seven years, shrinking industrial production had decreased by 40 % and foreign debt of initially about $ 8 billion had grown to more than $ 43 billion.

The new president Raul Alfonsin took over a country which had largely been de-industrialized and which was struggling with an inflation rate of several hundred percent. His attempt to solve economic problems in cooperation with the IMF met with bitter resistance from the working population. During his tenure, a wave of 4,000 strikes and 15 general strikes swept the country. Alfonsin issued a temporary wage and price freeze in agreement with the IMF and introduced a new currency, the "Austral", which was valid until the end of 1991. Fearing that he might be removed from office by the protesting masses, Alfonsin delayed the required lay-offs in the public service and only privatized three state-owned enterprises. In the eyes of the IMF, Alfonsin acted all too timidly, so the Fund and Western banks withdrew further loans, thus enforcing his resignation and placing their trust in his successor.

Their expectations were not disappointed. When Carlos Menem took over the presidency in July 1989, Argentina's per capita income was already almost 20 % below the level of 1975, and the standard of living of the working population had in many areas reached the level of a developing country. This, however, did not prevent Menem from joining forces with the IMF and implementing the most severe "shock program" that South America had experienced until then. The reforms of Economics Minister Domingo Cavallo, a Harvard graduate who

---

[24] The IMF was directly involved in this process. Dante Simone, an IMF staff member, worked as an advisor to the Central Bank during the dictatorship, giving its transactions his blessings.

had already served under the military as the director of the Central Bank, focused on the dismissal of hundreds of thousands of public employees, the elimination of all import barriers in the agricultural sector, the almost complete privatization of the banking sector, and the sale of state companies such as the airline Aerolineas Argentinas and the oil company YPF to foreign investors at very low prices.[25] The neoliberal agenda's scope by far surpassed the Chilean reforms under dictator Pinochet. In addition to a 50 % increase in VAT, which had a devastating effect especially on lower income groups, it involved pegging the peso to the dollar, a rise in interest and the commitment of the Central Bank, placed under control of the IMF, to back the Argentine currency with their dollar reserves at the ratio of 1:1.

The interest rate increase led financial institutions to borrow money at comparatively low interest rates in the dollar zone and lend it out at higher rates within Argentina – a procedure that even Milton Friedman, the guru of neoliberalism, labeled a "betrayal of the Argentinians". The pegging of the peso to the dollar created certainty for foreign investors and unleashed a true credit glut that led to rapid economic growth in 1991 and 1992, but at the same time significantly drove up Argentina's debt. For the export economy, the dollar peg of the peso, due to the remaining inflation and the overvaluation of the dollar, meant high or rising prices and a decrease in their competitiveness, while the domestic agricultural economy had to put up with declines in sales and production, unable to keep up with the competition from multinational corporations.

Milton Friedman

---

[25] YPF was purchased by the Spanish corporation Repsol, which from then on made half its operating profit in Argentina. Large parts of the Argentine water system were purchased by a French company conglomerate, which raised water prices in the provinces by up to 400 %.

Despite the foreseeable negative long-term consequences, the Menem government further advanced its program, rendering existing labor laws more flexible, lowering corporate tax rates (to 33 % versus 45 % in the US), nationalizing the debts of private companies, and converting the debt of state enterprises into foreign ownership under the "Brady Plan". The complete penetration of the economy by foreign capital worked like a drug: It promoted short-term growth and profits, but, in order to keep the economy going, continuously called for new capital, thus increasing Argentina's vulnerability to critical international developments. When the Mexican peso came under pressure in the so-called "tequila crisis"[26] in 1994 / 1995, the effects were felt immediately. Many foreign investors withdrew their money from Argentina; economic activity slumped to –0.1 %. Major banks reclaimed their loans, driving thousands of companies into bankruptcy. Smaller commercial banks collapsed, and unemployment shot up to 18 % within weeks.

The slump did not prevent the IMF from continuing to globally praise its "model pupil" Argentina as a textbook example of the effectiveness of structural adjustment programs. In fact, this came as no surprise, since international investors could rub their hands with glee: The sell-off of 40 % of Argentina's state-owned enterprises and 90 % of the nation's banks at crash prices had helped them rake in huge profits, while providing the Argentine government with revenues of $ 49 billion, with which foreign creditors were regularly serviced.

Neither the lenders nor the IMF cared about the fact that the new owners of the privatized enterprises turned their peso gains into hard currency at the Argentine Central Bank, and immediately transferred the money to North America or Europe, thus causing a steady currency drain which undermined the economy. They did not care either about the fact that at the end of Menem's term of office, 37 % of

---

[26] In January 1995 Mexico received loans in the amount of $ 47.8 billion (20 billion coming from the US), which were used to save major banks and investment funds and which drove the country's debt to new record levels.

the population lived in poverty, three quarters of them having been pushed below the poverty line only after the implementation of the neoliberal reforms. The IMF as well as the banks and major corporations only started to pay attention when revenue dropped dramatically in the two years before the turn of the millennium, and the budget deficit exploded after most lucrative parts of the Argentine family heirlooms had been sold off, and crises in East Asia, Russia, Brazil, and Turkey began to threaten the country, thus reducing the constant cash flow in their direction.

No country was hit harder by the economic and monetary crisis in Brazil than Argentina. When the fifth largest economy in the world unpegged its currency, the real, in January 1999, it lost 50 % of its value within a very short space of time. Argentine export goods, 30 % of which went to Brazil, became too expensive for buyers, while the now cheaper Brazilian products replaced domestic goods at home and on the world market. At the end of the 1990s, the soaring dollar caused the peso to appreciate due to its peg to the US currency, and thus prompted an additional price increase of Argentinian goods on the world market, as well as a price increase for foreign goods in the domestic market.

Fernando de la Rua, who succeeded Carlos Menem as president in October 1999, took over a country in recession whose public debt had grown to $ 114 billion, and which had to pay continually rising interest rates in order to raise fresh capital. As was customary in such situations, the IMF stepped in and offered a loan of $ 7.2 billion, conditional upon the reduction of the budget deficit within one year from $ 7.1 billion to $ 4.7 billion, i.e. conditional upon the enforcement of spending cuts amounting to $ 2.5 billion, mostly affecting the social sector – at a time when 14 out of 36 million Argentinians were already officially living below the poverty line.

When it became known in April 2000 that the government had approved cuts to the amount of $ 938 million per year – two thirds of them at the expense of wages and pensions for public employees – the anger of the population boiled over. On May 31, a crowd of 40,000 gathered outside the presidential palace to protest against the visit of an IMF delegation. The delegates turned a deaf ear to the protesters, continuing to negotiate and agreeing on new cuts to be implemented during the summer. Even these, however, could not prevent sovereign debt from increasing to $147 billion until the end of 2000. Again, the IMF stepped in and in cooperation with the government agreed on a "rescue package" in the amount of $ 39.7 billion ($ 13.7 billion from the IMF itself, $ 26 billion from other sources). In return, it demanded, among other things, the liberalization of the health sector, the deregulation of energy and telecommunications, an even more flexible labor market, more privatizations and a reduction in imports.

Working people opposed the measures, showing increasing resistance. In February 2001, thousands of unemployed in La Matanza, the city with the country's highest unemployment rate, assembled and marched to Buenos Aires. In March, President de la Rua, in response to the growing protests, formed a "government of national unity", and within three weeks appointed three finance ministers. The third, Menem's former minister Domingo Cavallo, announced immediately after taking office that international investors who kept "euro bonds" and "Brady bonds" would have to be given priority – even if that required further cuts to pensions that were below the subsistence minimum already.

Workers responded by blocking 22 streets leading to Buenos Aires in May 2001 and, from then on, closed down traffic on up to 50 highways across the country every day. The government stood firm and held its course unwaveringly with the backing of the IMF. In July, the Argentinian parliament granted Cavallo special powers and adopted the "zero deficit" law that forbade the government to spend more money than it collected in taxes. To raise urgently needed money, the government announced further budget cuts of $ 1.6 billion prior to the release of new government bonds. Instead of recognizing this as a sign of accommodation, investors assessed the measure as a sign of weakness, whereupon Argentina had to provide interest rates that were more than 50 % higher than planned, which accelerated the economic downturn dramatically.

At the end of the summer of 2001, production had decreased by 25 %. Thousands of businesses had to close down, one sixth of the working population was without jobs. A 40 % risk premium had to be paid on dollar loans on top of interest. The Central Bank lost $ 18 billion, i.e. half their deposits. The Government announced even tougher cuts, but failed to meet the budgetary requirements of the IMF, which then threatened to suspend payments – with the result that shortly afterwards, all hell broke loose.

Foreign banks withdrew hundreds of millions of dollars and deposited them in offshore havens. Working people, too, began to empty their bank accounts. Between November 28 and November 30 alone, 6 % of all savings, a total of $ 3.6 billion, were withdrawn. To stop the drain, the government closed the banks and froze accounts and assets. As of December 1, Argentine small investors were not allowed to withdraw more than $ 250 from their accounts – after major national and international speculators had already withdrawn and brought to safety more than $ 15 billion.

The government turned to the IMF for help but it did not respond favorably and even refused to pay out a due installment. A 24-hour general strike was called on December 13. Four days later, the government announced even tougher cuts of $ 9.2 billion, equaling about 18 % of their total budget. In the following days, hundreds of thousands flocked to the streets, surrounded ministries and the presidential palace and tried to make themselves heard as "cacerolazos" by beating on pots and pans. Although the protests were largely peaceful, the police used the sporadic lootings of food markets as a pretext to use violence against all demonstrators. Countless people were injured in street battles, about 2,000 protesters ended up in prison, and 31 died in the hail of police bullets. A spokesman for the IMF felt compelled to comment on the events in the style of Pontius Pilate: "The economic program in Argentina was designed by the Argentine government and the goal of eliminating the budget deficit was endorsed by the Argentine Congress," he said, trying to wash his hands in innocence by not mentioning with a single word the IMF's active involvement in Argentina's collapse.

108

The country descended into chaos. Angry protestors besieged the presidential palace for two days and fought fierce battles with the police. Fearing for their lives, President de la Rua and his minister of economic affairs fled by helicopter. Within two weeks, Congress appointed three different presidents. On December 23, Interim President Adolfo Rodriguez Saa announced to the world that Argentina was insolvent. On January 1, 2002, Congress installed Senator Eduardo Duhalde as president. Barely in office, he confirmed the biggest bankruptcy of all time and unpegged the peso from the dollar, as the currency reserves of the Central Bank were no longer sufficient to cover the huge demand. Within days, the peso lost 70 % of its value. The level of foreign debt and the prices of domestic loans exploded, while the flight of capital continued unabated.

Argentina had turned into a powder keg. Neighborhood committees were established, corporate facilities occupied by workers, and bankrupt enterprises taken over by them. In February Economics Minister Lenikov turned to IMF head Horst Köhler, urging him to release the funds that had been withheld in December. Lenikov was sent home without a cent, but ordered to continue increasing government revenue and to drastically reduce payments to the provinces.

Within three months a further 200,000 people lost their jobs, and industrial production fell by an additional 20 %. While debt service ate up 17 % of the Argentine state budget, the poverty rate reached 57 % and the unemployment rate went up to 23 %. Poverty-related diseases and malnutrition spread. In 2002, more than 20 % of children under five in the province of Tucumán were underweight. Despite these inhuman conditions, the IMF did not change its position. On the contrary, when the Argentine judiciary tried to stop the illegal withdrawal of huge amounts of dollars by foreign financial institutions and the hostile takeover of highly indebted state-owned enterprises by introducing new legislation, the IMF intervened and urged President Duhalde to veto both laws because they would "discourage foreign investment".

Obeying immediately, Duhalde went to even greater lengths in his subservience to the IMF. When taking office, he had promised to help domestic industry get back on its feet by restricting imports, returning dollar holdings to small savers and improving employment protection for industrial workers. Duhalde broke all three promises and fulfilled more IMF requirements in August. He fired the governor of San Juan because the latter defied his orders, forced provincial governors to sign a 14-point austerity program, gave the order to forcibly end factory occupations, and had insolvent tenants removed from their homes.

The fact that the once most prosperous country in South America had turned into a poorhouse for more than half the population and become a social nightmare for many of them within four years did not remain hidden from the eyes of the world. The role that the IMF had played met with harsh criticism. But, as so often, this criticism was defused and diluted by the media, and taken over by prominent "experts" whose primary purpose was to divert attention from the real causes of the disaster. Joseph Stiglitz, Economic Advisor to Bill Clinton from 1993 until 1997 and Chief Economist of the World Bank from 1997 until 2000, provided a telling example of this attitude, accusing the IMF of having made "a whole series of errors" in their exchange rate, in fiscal policies, and in the privatization process.

The idea that the IMF had "made mistakes" on the basis of misperceptions and inadequate analyses, thus unintentionally causing a social disaster, was utter nonsense. No other organization was as well-informed about Argentina's economy and its finances as the IMF. The Fund knew exactly what it was doing and what consequences its actions would have. A look at the results of the sovereign default, brought about with its support, shows that the IMF had remained absolutely faithful to the policy it had been following for years: favoring the economically powerful while disadvantaging the most vulnerable groups of society.

As it turned out, thousands of small bondholders who had purchased Argentine government securities[27] through investment funds now lost the majority of their deposits through a radical "haircut". While the IMF as well as the World Bank were exempt from this scheme, large foreign investors could also breathe a sigh of relief: The successor government under the new President Nestor Kirchner made sure that the bankruptcy "proceeded in an orderly fashion." Although the repayment term of their debt, due to the exchange of old bonds into new government bonds, was extended to a period of 42 years in June 2005, large foreign investors received an inflation compensation, a measure that was anything but customary.

The fact that Kirchner – just as his Brazilian counterpart Lula da Silva –presented himself as a harsh critic of the IMF, publicly holding it responsible for hunger and poverty in his country, was nothing but cheap populism and only served to mislead the public and prevent renewed social protests. Kirchner's finance Minister Miceli, who had already held a high post in the ministry of economy under Videla's regime of terror, clung to all the decisions made by her predecessor and in no way initiated a redistribution in favor of the working population or the poor. Kirchner's public tirades against the Fund did not prevent him from paying off all debts to the IMF prematurely at the end of 2005 and transferring $ 9.81 billion from the reserves of the Central Bank to the IMF's accounts.

---

[27] Solely in the euro zone, investment savers had invested 20 billion euros in Argentine government bonds.

Argentina's decision not to apply for any more loans from the IMF for the time being not only suited the IMF well; it was also arranged with its Director for the Western Hemisphere, A. Singh. Due to the increasing frequency of crises in Southeast Asia, Russia and Latin America, the IMF urgently needed a period of consolidation to restructure its finances and prepare for the future, because the world financial system was already beginning to display the first signs of the next major international crisis – the global financial crash of 2007 and 2008.

Globalization and Financialization:
The Driving Powers behind the IMF

The hostility that the IMF had incurred among working people and the poor in Southeast Asia, Eastern Europe and Latin America, prompted several governments other than that in Buenos Aires to strike increasingly critical tones towards the Fund. This change in direction, however, did not reveal any real opposition to its policies. It was only an attempt by the 'critics' to appear "progressive" – especially during election campaigns. Not a single government actually risked breaking with the IMF, and for good reason: Such a decision would have immediately cut it off from all international capital flows and quite certainly ushered in its end.[28]

Nevertheless, the international media and a number of self-proclaimed "experts" took up public criticism of the IMF with enthusiasm and predicted its "descent into irrelevance" or even its impending end. A significant number of organizations critical to the IMF joined in, thus helping to take the IMF out of the line of fire temporarily and letting the protests against it gradually subside, especially in Western industrialized countries. Why should one fight against an organization that was already doomed?

---

[28] The announcements of Venezuela's president Hugo Chavez in 2007 and 2012 were also nothing but populist demagogy – Venezuela remained a member of the IMF beyond his death and has regularly serviced its debt.

114

This assessment of the situation had nothing to do with reality. Both the bankers of Wall Street, as well as the boards of multinational corporations and the officials in the US Treasury were able to rub their hands with glee at the turn of the millennium. Despite the many crises in the eighties and nineties, the IMF had succeeded in recapturing markets which international capital had been deprived of for decades. It had provided investors with extremely high profits even in times of severe financial crises, and shown all skeptics who actually called the shots in economic and financial policy matters around the globe.

The question arising in view of these facts was basically not what caused the apparent weakness of the IMF, but what caused the immense abundance of power it had concentrated in its hands within half a century. How could it be that a financial organization with less than three thousand employees, most of them sitting at their desks in Washington, could possibly have achieved such a unique global position in the history of the world's economy? How could it have such a lasting impact on the lives of a significant proportion of humanity across all national boundaries?

The key to answering this question could not be found either in the structure of the IMF, nor in the personal composition of its governing bodies. Although the Fund recruited (and still recruits) most of its members from the alumni classes of elite universities in the US and in Europe, one cannot speak of strategic thinking or even intellectual or technical brilliance on the part of its staff. The IMF's forecasts on the economic development of countries often turned out to be wrong, and none of its leading economists had correctly predicted even a single major international crisis. More than once its interventions had shown that it reacted rather frantically to developments instead of planning and acting in a forward-looking and carefully thought-out manner. However, if its success was not due to its own capacities or the competence of its staff, then it could only be explained by its environment or the conditions under which it had been operating.

Indeed, the answer to this puzzle was to be found exactly here. These conditions had fundamentally changed since the founding of the IMF after World War II. The following factors, in particular, had contributed to this end: The dissolution of the Bretton Woods system, the rise of economic globalization and, along with it, the weakening of the international trade union movement, the restoration of capitalism in the Soviet Union and its satellite states, and the steadily increasing importance of the financial sector.

The dissolution of the Bretton Woods system, by unpegging the dollar from gold and the replacement of the dollar peg to other currencies by "floating" exchange rates in the early seventies, should actually have terminated the IMF's existence. However, by simply abandoning its original purpose and transforming itself into the world's "lender of last resort", and thus becoming a pioneer of neoliberal reforms, the IMF – and the World Bank – managed to assume a globally unrivalled position.

Globalization, which is the ever-increasing integration of economic and financial processes, helped consolidate and expand this unique position. While a large part of industrial production from leading industrial countries was outsourced particularly to Asia during the mid-seventies, the profits generated were for the most part transferred directly back to the leading industrial countries. The IMF's judgment played a crucial role for international capital searching for new global investment opportunities with regard to the countries' credit ratings and the assessment of their obedience towards the enforcement of neoliberal structural reforms. For large investors, the IMF to a certain extent became a global investment guide and an indicator for the security of their investments.

Another factor that turned out to be extremely important for international capital was the trade unions' adherence to their purely national orientation. While corporations were constantly internationalizing the industrial production process on a world scale, the leadership of the unions did nothing to organize their own struggle beyond national borders. Instead, they firmly held on to the concept of domestic "social partnership", trying to convince their members that workers and employers were "all in the same boat" and that it was outside competition that forced them to show restraint in domestic compensation and remuneration issues. Their readiness to make compromises paid off for union leaders. In return for keeping the peace, they were awarded memberships in supervisory boards and ministerial posts. For rank-and-file members, this development had fatal consequences, because their protests proved to be increasingly futile, and more and more members left the unions. This again played directly into the hands of the IMF, because the increasing weakness of the international labor movement enabled it to implement measures that it would have hardly been able to enforce in previous decades.

Although opening up a huge additional market for international financial capital, the restoration of capitalism in the Soviet Union and its satellite states was also associated with large uncertainties. The structures of central planning had to be abolished, private ownership of the means of production reintroduced, and its sustainability guaranteed. In fact, there was only one organization that had the necessary means of exerting pressure to enforce these measures, if necessary even against the will of the majority of the population, without resorting to military action: the IMF.

These three factors alone would have been sufficient to help the IMF to its undisputed global position. Still, a fourth was added, which turned out to be of paramount importance, particularly for the role of the IMF during the first decade of the 21st century: The increasing "financialization" of the world economy which had set in in the mid-seventies. This trend has led to an epochal restructuring of international capitalism, contributing greatly to the boom of the 1990s, and paving the way towards the burst of the dotcom bubble, the crash of the US housing market, the financial crisis of 2007 / 2008 and the euro crisis. It has shaped the face of the modern-day world, and understanding its history is indispensable for understanding the reorientation of the IMF towards Europe and its role in the "troika". Let us look at a few facts:

The United States' rise to world power before the Second World War was largely owed to the increasing importance of the financial sector. The most important motors of this development were the investment banks that ran high risks speculating with the deposits of their customers, often without their knowledge. The New York stock market crash of 1929, the subsequent global economic crisis and the Great Depression, which led to mass impoverishment in the United States, deprived many of these depositors – most of them working people, who in good faith had deposited their money in savings accounts – of all their assets and therefore aggravated their rage against the banks. In order to dampen the protests of the population and the trade unions, which were very strong then, newly elected Democratic President Franklin D. Roosevelt issued the second "Glass-Steagall Act", which established the separate banking system[29] in 1933, and in 1934 introduced the world's first stock exchange supervisory agency, the Securities and Exchange Commission (SEC).

These and several other legal regulations, which restricted financial capital's freedom of movement, while at the same time guaranteeing small investors and savers a certain level of security, remained largely untouched for about thirty years. When the end of the post-war boom loomed in the 1960s, the first voices were raised demanding a relaxation of these rules. In the 1970s, these voices increased both in numbers and volume, as economic growth, particularly in the industrialized nations, was slowing down, and the petrodollar glut required new investment opportunities.

---

[29] The »Glass Steagall Act" separated commercial banks for conventional deposit and credit business, which were considered reputable, from investment banks that were allowed to go on speculating and running high risks.

Gerald Ford, the unelected successor of ousted president Richard Nixon, was the first US president to completely subordinate his government to financial sector pressures. Ford made Nelson Rockefeller, billionaire and director of the *Federal Reserve Bank of New York*, his vice president and hired neoliberal economics professor Alan Greenspan as his economic advisor. After jointly lowering the profit tax on companies and the income tax for the rich, they allied themselves with the *Bank of America* and *Merrill Lynch* and began to weaken the provisions of the two-tier banking system.

In the 1980s, conservative British Prime Minister Margaret Thatcher and Republican US President Ronald Reagan went even further. By systematically liberalizing markets and deregulating the banking industry, they paved the way for an increasingly greater expansion of the financial sector, a policy that was continued under Thatcher's successor, Tony Blair, and Reagan's successors, Republican George Bush and Democrat Bill Clinton (who officially abolished the Glass-Steagall Act in 1999 and completely deregulated the derivatives[30] market in 2000).

The global centers of international high finance – Wall Street and the City of London – immediately capitalized on the liberties given to them. Within a few years, a shadow banking system of hedge funds (trusts of billionaires that generated profits unheard of previously) and investment firms emerged. They were able to run almost unlimited risks, since although acting like banks, they were not subject to their statutory restrictions. Furthermore, an increasing number of new financial products were invented or refined. In particular, the trade of purely financial instruments such as derivatives, which had nothing to do with the real economy (the production of goods) exploded and multiplied the risks of transactions by "leveraging" (and thus multiplying risk and potential debt). The reintroduction of short sales, which

---

[30] Derivatives are forward transactions, which originally served as a hedge against risks, but, with the rise of financialization, were increasingly used for speculation.

US President Ronald Reagan and
British Prime Minister Margaret Thatcher, 1984

had been banned in the US in the 1930s, allowed investors to once again bet on falling prices.

Accompanied by the information technology revolution and the introduction of computer-based exchange trading, the explosion of the financial system led to an orgy of speculation, also called "casino capitalism", which by far exceeded all previously known varieties of personal enrichment. It allowed for astronomical profits within very short spaces of time, and led to the increasing replacement of corporate profits coming from the real economy by profits stemming from the financial industry. The turnover in international foreign exchange trading, at $ 70 billion per day in 1970, shot up to $ 590 billion in 1989 and reached around $ 1,250 billion per day in 2001. Profits from the financial sector, made by multinational corporations based in the US, which had stood at 10 % in 1980, reached 40 % a quarter century later.

Apart from this basic change in the character of the system, the merging of old and new money led to another phenomenon which until that time had been unknown in the history of capitalism: the unprecedented concentration of assets in the hands of a tiny group of multi-billionaires. It gave rise to a "financial aristocracy" of several hundred individuals and families, who, due to their fabulous wealth, have meanwhile become the most powerful international force in all walks of life, dominating and controlling not only trade, production and finance, but also all other sectors of society. In contrast to the medieval aristocracy, the rule of this layer, called "Ultra High Net Worth" (UHNW) individuals in banking parlance, is not geographically restricted, but global. UHNW individuals exercise their power primarily by manipulating the "financial markets" through the financial institutions which they control to influence share and commodity prices by forcing governments to appreciate or depreciate currencies or, in case of non-compliance, by chasing them out of office and thus forcing entire states to their knees.[31]

The wealth of UHNW individuals, most of whom live in the US (which also has the largest financial market and the US Federal Reserve, the world's most powerful financial weapon), has been progressively increasing at an unprecedented pace since the 1990s. It more than doubled between 2009 and 2012 from $ 3.1 to $ 6.5 trillion and in 2013 approximately equaled the total gross domestic product of all countries of the world except China and the US.

UHNW individuals live largely withdrawn and prefer to operate undetected. Like puppeteers they not only dominate global economic events as owners of banks, hedge funds, insurance companies and transnational corporations, but, due to their ownership of the global

---

[31] Just one example: In 1992 billionaire George Soros together with others bet against die British pound, provoking a 25% devaluation against the American dollar. Almost causing the collapse of the European monetary system, Soros raked in a profit of more than $ 1 billion.

media, also determine the image of reality which is conveyed to people all over the world (and which, of course, obscures their true role). By means of their foundations they help finance elite universities such as Harvard and Stanford, where those selected to represent their interests in the future are educated, and entertain think tanks where political strategies, directly tailored to their needs, are developed. They determine which politicians may represent their interests by financing election campaigns, and enforce the implementation of their strategies by applying pressure on the financial markets. They subordinate all economic and social matters to their one and only aim, which is to increase their wealth. They make up the richest and economically most powerful group of people that ever existed on this planet, and one of the most important power instruments they rely on is the IMF.

The Financial Crisis of 2007 / 2008 and the IMF: The Calm before the Storm

Before the turn of the millennium, globalization brought more than a billion new workers to the labor market in Asia, enabling international corporations to drastically reduce their labor costs. Workers in the industrialized countries, however, were not allowed to participate in the corporations' rise in profit by means of wage increases and an expansion of social benefits as they had in the 1950s and 1960s. On the contrary, employers used outsourcing of jobs, rising unemployment in Europe and the United States, and starvation wages paid abroad to exert increasing pressure on workers in collective bargaining, threatening that excessive demands would lead to a further transfer of even more jobs to low-wage countries. Starting with the new millennium, this intransigent attitude of employers initiated a decline in the standard of living of the working population in Europe and the US, which had already stagnated between 1980 and 2000.

The decrease in purchasing power confronted finance capital with a serious problem, because capitalism requires incessant growth, based on constant sales of the goods produced. But how could people with less and less money in their pockets be encouraged to buy more and more products? Capitalism provides a solution for this problem, but once again, it benefits solely the financial sector: In order to bridge a "financing gap", banks provide the working population with credit which, of course, has to be repaid. But credit calls for collateral. Where was this to come from if people earned less and less?

The magic formula of the global economy at the dawn of the new millennium was the US housing market. The world's largest and most profitable real estate market was in an upward trend that had lasted for years, with apparently no end in sight. If a bank secured a loan with a mortgage (lien) on a house under conditions of steadily rising house prices, it ran basically no risk: If the borrower became insolvent, the bank could initiate foreclosure proceedings, pursue enforcement, and then sell the house, which had meanwhile gone up in value, at a higher price.

This scheme proved so lucrative that banks even extended it to customers they had previously rejected: people who had fallen victim to forced expropriations, gone bankrupt, or defaulted on mortgage payments in the past and thus fell into the "subprime" segment, were once again considered credit-worthy. In this way, a true avalanche of home purchases was unleashed, at the end of which subprime buyers, due to the keen competition among lenders, had to offer almost no collateral. As it was clear that this house of cards had to collapse at some point, the banks quickly shifted the risk from one financial institution to another, resorting to "asset securitization", i.e. bundling their credit claims and selling them in international financial markets.

This, however, by no means meant the end of the line for profiteering. Even risk could be turned into money. Before passing it on to someone else, all one had to do was to cover it by so-called credit default swaps[32], which Wall Street banker Blythe Masters had invented in 1994. And even such manipulations could be still be topped: anyone who wanted to jump on the carousel without owning loan securitizations merely had to purchase credit default swaps and could thus place bets on transactions which they themselves were not involved in.

---

[32] Credit default swaps are used by financial institutions not only to insure themselves against the risk of non-repayment of loans, but also to remove risks from their balance sheets.

Banks and financial institutions around the world jumped at the opportunity and entered the business on a grand scale. Accompanied by a sort of gold rush mood, the scope of globally concluded credit default swap contracts kept breaking new records[33], until in 2006 the US housing market passed its peak and prices began to fall while interest rates at the same time began to rise. The downward spiral quickly turned into a torrent and triggered an unprecedented global chain reaction. The insolvency of many US homeowners led to a rapid loss in the value of securitized loans, turning them into "toxic" (= worthless) securities, and tearing huge holes into the balance sheets of major banks around the world. Credit default swaps matured to an unexpected extent and generated a crisis that has often been compared to the Great Depression of the 1930s.

As striking as the parallels between the two crises are, it was the differences between them that were decisive. The crisis in the 1930s had not only led to huge economic and financial losses, but also caused serious disagreements between nation states, which eventually sparked off World War II. The reason for this was that at the time, financial capital was more widely spread and tied considerably more strongly to nation-state structures than 75 years later. Although already representing the interests of banks, financial institutions, and large corporations, governments in the 1930s had considerably more room for maneuvering than today and usually aimed for national solutions for their problems. This ultimately led them to try to increase their own country's sphere of influence by using military force (at the expense of the lives of some 70 million people) in order to provide their own financial capital with new investment and sales opportunities.

The financial crisis that began in 2007 unfolded under completely different conditions. Globalization and financialization had led to a fusion of international finance capital during the past quarter of a cen-

---

[33] Global derivatives trading amounted to around $ 680 billion in December 2007, according to a report by the *Bank for International Settlements*.

tury, which in turn had caused an unprecedented concentration of wealth and power in the hands of the financial aristocracy. When the crisis suddenly spread out to a large number of other countries from its center in the United States, and it gradually became clear what gigantic sums could be lost, the community of multi-billionaires took a clear decision. They called for a campaign that was not directed against individual countries, but against working people, pensioners and small investors all over the world. These were to foot the bill and pay for the losses threatening the financial aristocracy. This campaign was not to be fought with arms, but by a maneuver that was unprecedented in the history of mankind – the largest redistribution of wealth ever seen on this planet.

The plan was strategically prepared by a quickly organized campaign focusing on the notion of "too big to fail". The international media financed by the financial aristocracy thus took on the task of brainwashing the public in the United States and in Europe by convincing them that certain banks and financial institutions were "systemically indispensable" and needed to be saved at all costs. They claimed that their fall would lead to a collapse of the entire system, which in turn would usher in the downfall of civilization or at least create conditions comparable to those of the Great Depression of the 1930s. This argument was not even completely false. As the crash of *Lehman Brothers* had shown, the collapse of a single bank could, due to its global interconnections, actually destabilize the entire system. However, the campaign's actual objective was to systematically obscure the origin of the money that was to be used to save the "too-big-to-fail" institutions. It was not to come from those who in previous years had filled their pockets by unrestrained speculation and were sitting on cash reserves in the trillions. Instead, it was the governments that were to step in – with the taxpayers' money. In other words, the wealthy owners of banks and financial institutions, who had lost money betting on the wrong horse, were to be compensated with the hard-earned money of the working population – not directly, but via the tax-collecting agencies of the state.

Public reaction to the campaign showed how powerful the financial aristocracy had become. There was virtually no significant opposition – neither by parliaments nor by political parties or trade unions. It was as if the whole world bowed to the reasoning of "too big to fail". When the first large sums from taxpayers' money were actually used to secure the wealth of the financial aristocracy, there was no resistance at all.[34]

Hundreds of billions of dollars changed hands. In the US, market giants such as real estate financiers Freddie Mac and Fannie May and insurer AIG were taken over by the state, their owners thus spared huge losses. In Switzerland, the bank UBS, which had posted a profit of 5.6 billion Swiss francs in the second quarter of 2007 alone, received a government infusion of almost 60 billion Swiss francs overnight, without prior discussion in parliament and without any parties or unions taking to the streets in protest afterwards – in a country that boasts of its direct democracy through plebiscites!

While Great Britain, Germany, France, Belgium, Luxembourg, the Netherlands and many other countries pumped huge sums into the rescue of individual financial institutions, the financial aristocracy took advantage of the situation and also capitalized on it in other respects. Big American banks in particular used chaotic market conditions and bought dozens of ailing savings banks, smaller banks and companies at rock bottom prices. The fact that *Lehman Brothers*, although "too big to fail", was driven into bankruptcy, was mainly due to the fact that Treasury Secretary Henry Paulson was a former *Goldman Sachs* banker doing his very best to make his ex-employer come out of the crisis as one of its major beneficiaries. The greatest profiteer, however, was the financial aristocracy, which as a whole not only made no losses, but greatly enriched itself during the crisis and was able to even lay

---

[34] The protest movement Occupy Wall Street was only established in October 2011.

the foundation for an almost exponential increase in its wealth after the crisis.

Still, there were new and bigger problems ahead. The governments' strategy of using taxpayers' money to save banks and financial institutions that threatened to be pulled into the abyss after the *Lehman* crash worked out in Switzerland and in several large EU countries, because these states had enough money to fill the resulting budget holes after the rescue operation. But what if such a hole was larger than the state budget? What would happen if an overburdened state went bankrupt? Would it actually lead to the much-feared chain reaction and a total collapse of the world financial system?

What at first glance looked like a chronic pessimist's game of make-believe was soon to become a very realistic threat, looming on the horizon of the world financial system only three weeks after the fall of *Lehman Brothers*. Located in the midst of the North Atlantic, a tiny and hitherto economically completely insignificant country, as a result of the *Lehman* crash, was threatened by precisely this fate and had to be rescued in a most dramatic overnight operation executed by an international financial alliance under the leadership of the IMF.

Iceland's Banking Crash of 2008:
The IMF Turns its Eye on Europe

Due to its isolation and its small population of only about 300,000, until the beginning of this century, Iceland was one of the internationally least significant countries in Europe. That changed abruptly when the collapse of the Icelandic banking system alarmed the international public in the fall of 2008. The subsequent intervention of the IMF attracted global attention and enabled the whole world to see how life in one of the richest countries in the world[35] took a tragic turn for the worse.

The events on the island in the Nordic Seas marked the culmination of developments that had set in a quarter of a century earlier. At that time Iceland's ruling families started to realize what opportunities emerging from globalization and financialization were escaping them. In order to overcome their isolation from the rest of the world and participate in the gold rush of global casino capitalism, they started urging their government to open up Iceland's economy to international financial markets in the late 1980s. When David Oddsson was elected Prime Minister in 1991, they finally found an open ear.

Oddsson, an ardent admirer of Ronald Reagan and Margaret Thatcher, implemented a set of neoliberal reforms entirely to the taste of the IMF. He privatized state-owned enterprises, and increased taxes on

---

[35] Average income in Iceland in 2007 was about $ 70,000, i.e. 1.6 times as high as that in the US.

small and medium income, while lowering corporate taxes by more than 50 % and deregulating trade and finance. The economy responded with a powerful upswing, turning some members of the Icelandic financial elite such as Bjorgolfur Gudmundsson, the later owner of British soccer club West Ham United, into billionaires.

In 2002 and 2003, the government privatized the country's three largest banks. Contrary to all public assurances of intending to diversify holdings, a 48.5 % share of the largest bank went to the asset management company of three billionaires close to the government, who owed a large part of their fortunes to the restoration of capitalism in Russia. The new owners returned the favor by awarding several senior positions at the bank to members of the ruling coalition parties.

The chairman of the privatization committee of the banks left the panel in protest. The fact that his publicly expressed allegations of favoritism and corruption did not have any legal consequences was a clear indication of how much the neoliberal privatization process had already changed the balance of power between the Icelandic state and the wealthy clans in favor of the latter.

With the full backing of the government, the new owners of the banks immediately embarked on an aggressive expansion strategy, which literally led to an explosion of Iceland's financial system. Share prices on the stock exchange, manipulated by the banks through pre-arranged mutual purchases from 2003 until 2007, rose at a globally unparalleled rate of 42.7 % per year, while prices for houses and flats more than doubled within six years. By the end of 2003, the country's mountain of debt had increased to twice the gross domestic product, reaching seven times its level in 2007. In June 2008, the country's total debt amounted to almost ten times the GDP – slightly more than 50 billion euros, or 160,000 euros per capita of Iceland's population.

As early as 2006, a number of European financial institutions began to doubt the repayment ability of the Icelandic banks, as the formation of bubbles on the Icelandic stock and property market became increasingly obvious and the level of debt by far exceeded the operational resources of the Icelandic Central Bank.[36] Hesitant lending from Europe, however, did not prompt the Icelandic banks to rethink their course. On the contrary: they called in the government and the Chamber of Commerce, which in turn, with the support of purchased expertise, reaffirmed the soundness of the system and intensified their efforts in the search for less critical foreign donors. They actually managed to find them on the US bond market and among private and public investors, especially in Germany, England and the Netherlands. After quickly establishing online banks such as the infamous "Icesave" bank, they offered up to 6 % interest on call money and collected over 6.5 billion euros from hundreds of thousands of savers – more than half the sum total of Iceland's gross domestic product.

The money raised was immediately loaned to Icelandic entrepreneurs who indiscriminately invested it in domestic corporations, international fashion retailers, British soccer teams, Danish free newspapers, and American and Scandinavian supermarkets. As rapid domestic growth fueled inflation, the Central Bank of Iceland tried to counteract by increasing its interest rate. This in turn attracted foreign investors who profited through currency speculation, while an increasing number of Icelandic households, due to the favorable conditions in foreign currencies such as the Swiss franc or the Japanese yen, took on more and more debt.

Due to the critical development in the US and its negative impact on the rest of the world, the threat of a collapse became increasingly obvious in the spring of 2008. As the Asian financial crisis had shown ten years earlier, speculators who relied on quick profits were easy to scare and tended to withdraw their "hot money" abruptly in times of crisis.

---

[36] The ratio of short-term foreign debt to the Central Bank's foreign reserves, the critical limit of which is generally indicated at 1:1, had already reached a level of 8:1 in Iceland in 2006.

However, the point of no return had already been reached. Without the constant influx of foreign money, the exchange rate of the krona, which had already fallen sharply, could no longer be stabilized. A further depreciation, however, had to be prevented, because economic growth was already stalling due to a rise in import prices, and it would have threatened the solvency of the Icelandic banks due to the massive amount of debt in foreign currencies that many citizens had incurred. Iceland's banks, with the strong support of the government, had maneuvered the country into a desperate situation.

While the vast majority of Icelanders more or less unsuspectingly went about their work and neither media nor politics warned of the oncoming financial tsunami, things certainly looked different on Wall Street and in the City of London. Top bankers, financial brokers and hedge fund managers in the control centers of international finance knew very well that their time had come, and began repositioning themselves for the impending collapse. The crises of recent years in Asia and South America had taught them that there was hardly a more favorable opportunity for raking in huge profits than a national financial crash.

With cold-blooded calculation, they started to take out bets on the collapse of Iceland's banks and began to meticulously scrutinize the country's economy in order to be able to intervene at the decisive moment and grab huge pieces of real estate at bargain prices, purchase securities downgraded to junk status, or get their hands on mineral resources released for sale at rock bottom prices by the state. Planning security was provided by a reliable partner that they could be sure would do everything in its power to create the conditions for their foray: the IMF.

Indeed, they did not have to wait long. The bankruptcy of the fourth-largest US investment bank *Lehman Brothers* brought international payment flows to a standstill in September 2008 and had an immediate effect on Iceland. When one of the three major Icelandic banks was no longer able to raise fresh funds at the end of September, ex-Prime Minister David Oddsson, who after nearly 14 years as head of government had changed into the executive suite of the Icelandic Central Bank, came to its help. The acquisition of 75 % of the bank's shares by the state, however, had the opposite effect of what Oddsson had intended: It undermined the already battered confidence in the Icelandic financial system and triggered a bank run. Within days, the entire Icelandic banking system collapsed, stock prices plummeted, and the exchange rate of the krona fell by more than 25 %. To avert national bankruptcy, the government, in a hastily convened special meeting, adopted emergency legislation, took over control of the three largest banks on the instructions of the IMF, and immediately denied foreign customers access to their accounts.

The British government responded on the very same day. Accompanied by hate-filled tirades against the Icelandic government and with reference to their "anti-terrorist" legislation (Prime Minister Gordon Brown saw the British banking system acutely threatened by Iceland's "hostile act" of account blocking), it froze all deposits of Icelandic online banks, fully disbursed domestic depositors out of fear of a bank run in the UK, but ultimately reclaimed the money, including interest, threatening legal action against Iceland. Reykjavik answered by declaring that the Icelandic government and its central bank simply did not have the money. Seeking help, Iceland turned to the IMF.

For IMF officials who had been following events on the island with a critical eye since 2006,[37] Iceland presented a special case in several respects. On the one hand, it was the first time in thirty years that a European government demanded a loan from the IMF. On the other hand, Iceland ran the highest public debt (in relation to GDP the IMF had ever dealt with. Furthermore, it was the first international mission after the outbreak of the subprime mortgage crisis in the United States, the consequences of which acutely threatened the entire global finan-

---

[37] In a report of 13 July, 2006, the IMF had already established that the pace of growth of the Icelandic financial system made it "vulnerable to attack" and "undermined its health".

cial system. That meant that the Icelandic banking crisis had to be isolated and resolved as quickly and as effectively as possible. In other words, a tough program was necessary which certainly would not be easy to enforce because of the expected resistance from the population.

Retrospective reports and assessments of the Icelandic crisis often lead people to believe that the country actually put up a struggle against global finance capital and successfully defied it. Numerous articles claim that Iceland, against the advice of the IMF, did not save its banks, but let them go bankrupt, later on even holding those found guilty for the country's plight accountable.

Although these assumptions are completely false, there are good reasons for such misconceptions: Iceland at that time was at the center of world attention and it soon became clear that its population was not willing to accept a sudden and dramatic deterioration of its living standards without putting up a fight. Pictures showing angry citizens rebelling against their own government as victims of greedy profit-seeking bankers went around the world and created an extremely critical mood for financial capital which, due to the global nature of the financial crisis, threatened to spill over to other countries. In order to avert this danger and to neutralize the effects of the protests in Iceland, the IMF and the government in Reykjavik resorted to a measure that had already proven itself in South America: They deceived the public by simulating a conflict which actually did not exist.

While the government publicly condemned the IMF, its members seemingly defending themselves against interference from outside, the strings were actually jointly pulled in the background, strictly according to the IMF's plan. To those who did not allow themselves to be blinded by the ideological maneuvers of those involved, but looked at the facts objectively, the situation was clear: the Icelandic government had only reined in the banks as far as had been absolutely essential due to the size of their losses. Other than that, it had done everything in its power to compensate their creditors.

Even when the Icelandic president, facing increasing popular protests and seeking to prevent an open uprising, refused to sign a law compensating foreign investors, the government did not back him.[38] The alleged prosecution of the perpetrators of the crisis on closer inspection also turned out to be a hoax: After being taken to court, Prime Minister Geir Haarde was acquitted, and only a few subordinates received extremely mild sentences. Whoever was not put on probation was later given early release. None of the defendants had to repay the partly significant sums they had usurped during the boom.

135

The way things developed after the crash clearly revealed that Iceland had not embarked on its "own way out of the crisis". Only a few days later, the IMF committed itself to providing a stand-by loan of $ 2.1 billion. With a fixed maturity period of two years, it was to be paid in nine tranches and subjected to regular progress tests. The release of the first tranche was linked to the condition that Iceland's government officially recognize all foreign debt and commit itself to its repayment on a contractually binding basis. The release of all other tranches was linked to the condition that the government undertake every effort to attract foreign investors and refrain from doing whatever might deter them. This, among others, comprised strict environmental regulations and high taxes. A 10 % cut in the budgets of all ministries led to the cancellation of public funds for hospitals, schools and kindergartens, and marked the starting signal for the dismantling of what until then had been one of Europe's best social systems.

When Iceland's Central Bank, in order to boost the country's economy, lowered the interest rate from 15.5 % to 12 % on October 14, 2008 without previously consulting the IMF, the Fund showed its teeth. It ordered the Central Bank to reverse its decision immediately, and two weeks later forced it to raise the interest rate by 2 % to 18 %, thus im-

---

[38] The Icelandic government had declared itself willing to accept a regulation according to which foreign debt was to be paid off at an interest rate of 3 % over the course of 35 years.

plementing a measure that put domestic enterprises at an even greater disadvantage in relation to foreign hedge funds and major banks. The three large banks which the state had taken over during the crisis were re-privatized along with the savings banks.

While the losses that were made, including the three billion euros that the Icelandic pension fund had gambled away through risky speculation, were to be borne exclusively by Icelandic taxpayers, managers of hedge funds could at the same time rub their hands with glee. They had exploited the feeling of insecurity among many investors who had been afraid of losing their entire deposits when the banks began to collapse, and bought their bonds at rock bottom prices when the crisis set in. Now they used exactly these bonds to secure themselves a considerable share in the new banks, thus bringing the Icelandic banking system largely under their control.

The case of HS Orka demonstrates under what conditions state enterprises were sold. 98.5 % of the power company, which specializes in the utilization of geothermal energy, was sold to the Canadian company Magma Energy (known as Alterra since its fusion with Plutonic Power Corporation in 2011). Public indignation and even Icelandic pop singer Björk's campaign against the deal, which received worldwide attention, did not keep the government and the IMF from conceding the company usage rights over a period of 65 years with an option for a further 65 years – way into the year 2140!

While hedge funds, major banks and multinational corporations targeted everything that looked even remotely profitable, working people suffered blow after blow. First of all, they lost a huge mountain of savings. With Iceland being a member of the *European Economic Area* (EEA), the deposit guarantee scheme for banks was regulated by the provisions of the EU, which provided for a maximum reimbursement of only 20,887 euros per savings deposit. Many families were deprived of the fruits of years of work; old people lost a large part of their retirement savings. But there was more: Since most loans were linked to inflation or had been taken out in foreign currencies, the sums that had to be repaid increased considerably.

The collapse of the stock and the bond market, in which many had put their savings, largely erased these financial reserves. Many homeowners faced increasing hardships, so that the government found itself constrained to limit their debt. Capping the maximum value of mortgages at 110 % of the home value, however, was not a humanitarian measure, but only the deliberately calculated attempt by the government to control popular anger and help creditors keep the number of personal bankruptcies as low as possible.

At a time when unemployment soared from 1 % to 9 % and in combination with a sharp recession exerted considerable pressure on the general level of wages, private household debt rose to about 11,000 euros per capita. During the first months after the collapse about 8,000 able-bodied and mostly well-educated Icelanders saw no future for themselves and, just as many foreign workers, left the country. One percent of the population was no longer able to support themselves and had to be cared for in canteen kitchens run by the Salvation Army. The restrictions in education and health care, in which the principle of supplementary compensation was introduced, reduced people's quality of life just as much as personal limitations brought about by maintaining capital controls, which for years allowed Icelanders the exchange of crowns into foreign currencies only in exceptional cases.

Altogether, the policies of the IMF have transformed Iceland, whose standard of living was among the highest in the world, into a low-wage country whose future generations of citizens will even have to pay off debt for which they bear no responsibility. They have also turned a largely indigenous, self-contained economy into one that today is dominated by hedge funds, which have long since drawn it back into the speculation carousel of international finance capital, and made it a pawn in the hands of powers which it could not control even if it wanted to.

The fact that things became relatively quiet around Iceland soon after the crash was mainly due to the fact that simultaneously, a crisis was brewing in several European countries. Also caused by the enrichment orgy of the wealthy and accompanied by neoliberal policies of austerity, its consequences for the working population would surpass anything the continent had seen since World War II.

Ireland and the IMF:
Causing an Explosion of Poverty

Ireland's economy experienced an unprecedented boom between 1995 and 2007. Named the "Celtic Tiger" with reference to the Asian "Tiger States" of the 1980s and 90s, the boom provided the country with average growth rates of 7.4 % over a period of 12 years. It reduced unemployment, led to an improvement of infrastructure, transformed one of the lowest per-capita incomes in Europe into the second highest, and turned a classic emigration country into a country of immigration.

The advocates of neoliberalism celebrated Ireland's success as definitive proof that their concepts of liberalization, deregulation and privatization were effective. Although the gap between rich and poor grew steadily throughout the boom,[39] the average income of ordinary workers doubled within one and a half decades and was seen by the neoliberal community as a confirmation of their "trickle-down" principle, which stipulates that in a booming economy, a portion of the profits of the rich "trickles down" to the poor.

Ireland's rapid development was made possible by a combination of several factors. Entry to the European Community in 1973 gave the country access to the European market and opened it up for foreign investors. In the 1980s and 90s, employers, the government, and the unions, in the name of "collective partnership", joined forces and

---

[39] According to the United Nations, social inequality in Ireland in 2004 was second only to the United States among Western nations.

concluded four three-year-agreements which curbed wages, restricted benefits, made it more difficult to call strikes and facilitated the "flexibilization" of working hours. In addition, wage increases were largely replaced by tax concessions.

The new rules were especially attractive to American IT companies such as Dell, Intel, Apple, Google and Microsoft. The gradual reduction of the corporate tax, which had stood at 40 % in 1995, to 12.5 % in 2003, the introduction of a reduced tariff of 10 % for production facilities inside the country, and subsidies from the EU budget, provided corporations with massive competitive advantages internationally and led to a veritable immigration wave of foreign companies. The option of additionally reducing an already extremely low tax burden by the tax-friendly accounting of foreign profits ("Double Irish with a Dutch sandwich"[40]) led numerous location-bound US and European companies to register in Ireland for tax purposes.

Another crucial factor in Ireland's meteoric rise was the complete lack of any effective banking supervision. Although the EU and its predecessor organization EC knew of this situation, they did not oppose it or call for the introduction of a supervisory authority. On the contrary: Immediately after its establishment in 1993, the EU went out of its way to support the establishment of a financial oasis in Ireland. Many European companies seized the opportunity with both hands and from then on conducted their tax-privileged transactions mainly through Dublin. Major banks founded dozens of "special purpose entities", thus outsourcing high-risk speculative transactions to Ireland – a development that prompted the New York Times to label Ireland the "Wild West of European finance".

---

[40] Legal sleight of hand that enables global enterprises to lower their tax burden by 80 % to 90 % by taking advantage of loopholes in taxation laws in Ireland and the Netherlands.

In order to profitably invest speculative gains, bank capital from the mid-nineties on increasingly turned to the Irish property market. With the support of the government, which favored the project by tax reductions, a massive amount of loans was made available to the commercial sector and to private households, effecting a tripling of the annual rate of completion of apartments and houses between 1995 and 2006. In 2004 alone, 80,000 new apartments and houses were built – 7.5 times as much per capita as in the UK. As property prices rose dramatically (quadrupling between 1996 and 2006), more and more potential buyers turned up at the banks asking for credit.[41]

The development harbored several risks. On the one hand, the Irish state's share in tax revenues kept rising, making it increasingly dependent on the construction sector. On the other hand, Irish banks had to steadily lower acceptance criteria when granting new loans to their debtors. Just as in the US, risk kept increasing for both sides with every new contract. When the world financial crisis reached Ireland in 2007 / 2008, it hit a minefield.

Within a year, both the speculative bubble in the financial market as well as the real estate bubble burst and jointly triggered a chain reaction: Scores of companies were shut down or left the country, unemployment soared, medium-sized enterprises and private households were unable to service their loans, and real estate prices collapsed. As the global crisis made it impossible for Irish banks to refinance on the capital market, the Irish banking system came under severe pressure.

The government in Dublin responded by issuing a general guarantee on deposits at six major Irish financial institutions on September 30, 2008. It was an absurd promise, as the sum total of 485 billion euros equaled 2.7 times the Irish GDP, by far exceeding the financial resources of the government, but it was an important signal to interna-

---

[41] Estate-related loans between 2002 und 2008 accounted for almost 80 % of growth in total lending in Ireland.

tional finance capital: major banks and hedge funds could from then on be sure that the state and thus the tax-paying people would pay for their losses.

It did not take long for the Irish Government to follow words with deeds. On January 21, 2009, the cabinet in Dublin nationalized the Anglo-Irish Bank and helped out its investors with a cash injection of 48.5 billion euros from public tax funds, thus redirecting funds that had been generated by the working population straight into the pockets of private shareholders.

But that was not the end of it. In order to consolidate public finances, the Irish parliament passed four austerity budgets in 2010, all serving one and the same purpose: to fully pass on the burden of the bank rescue to working people by lowering their long-term living standards. Public sector infrastructure projects were stopped, salaries reduced, jobs slashed, and severe budget cuts carried out in education and health care. Medium-income homeowners were amongst those who were hit hardest by the government's measures. Many of them could no longer service their mortgages and were therefore faced with forced expropriation and foreclosure by exactly those banks that had been rescued with their tax money!

At the same time attempts were made to rescue the ailing financial institutions through the establishment of a state-run "bad bank". The hastily arranged bailout, which cost Irish taxpayers a further 30 billion euros through the acquisition of "toxic" (worthless) securities, failed because the financial risks were unmanageable, but boosted national debt, which had stood at 43.9 % at the end of 2008, to 64.0 % at the end of 2009, thus further aggravating the situation.

In June 2010, the mountain of government debt reached a total of 530 billion euros, 369 billion euros thereof owed to European creditors. In November, even the last budget surpluses accumulated during the past decade were exhausted, while the nationalized Anglo-Irish Bank, with a loss of 17.7 billion euros for that year, faced the highest annual loss of a company in the history of Ireland. When rumors started spreading that Ireland was heading for national bankruptcy, Irish Prime Minister Cowen turned to the EU and the IMF on November 21, 2010 and asked for help.

Dominique Strauss-Kahn, 2007

Both organizations immediately called in the ECB and jointly decided that a bankruptcy had to be prevented at all costs, as otherwise banks in Germany, France and the US would have faced the risk of collapse (outstanding debt of German banks alone amounted to over 110 billion euros in Ireland). IMF chief Dominique Strauss-Kahn set the course for the alleged "relief campaign", saying that life would become more difficult for the working people of Ireland, because "it is hard for people when they must make sacrifices in favor of budget austerity."

What sacrifices Strauss-Kahn, closely collaborating with the EU and the ECB, meant became apparent when the conditions for an 85-billion-euro bail-out loan were released, to which the IMF contributed 22.5 billion euros, while 17.5 billion euros were taken from the Irish pension reserve fund. The program, designed to span a period of three years, among others comprised the following provisions:

- Cancellation of 24,750 jobs (8 % of total jobs) in the public service,

- Reduction of starting wages in the civil service by 10%,

- Reduction of social benefits for large families, e.g. decreasing the child allowance by ten euros per child per month,

- Reduction of social benefits for the unemployed,

- Raising of the wage tax, thus lowering the average income of industrial workers by around 1,400 euros per year,

- Reduction of the health budget,

- Freezing pensions in the public sector and progressively reducing them by an average of 4%,

- A gradual increase of the retirement age by three years to 68 in 2014, 2021, and 2028,

- Abolition of tax relief on private pension provision,

- An increase in taxation on cars, alcohol, and tobacco,

- Raising of VAT from 21 % to 23 % in 2014,

- Introduction of a property tax, affecting 50 % of households which had previously been tax-exempt,

- Loosening of regulations allowing financially troubled companies to withhold or only partially pay wages,

- Lowering of the minimum wage by 11 % from 8.65 euros to 7.65 euros.

While the measures reduced the Irish working people's standard of living for years to come, they did not touch the extremely low corporate tax rate of 12.5 %. Banks and corporations that had made huge profits in previous years were not asked to contribute to austerity; on the contrary: They were given the opportunity of raising money from the ECB at an interest rate of one percent, with which they could purchase government bonds, collateralized by the emergency funds, thus creating new sources of profit for themselves. The downgrading of Ireland's credit-worthiness by US rating agency Moody's also came as a godsend to major American banks, enabling them to demand higher rates for their credit default swaps. Interest for IMF and EU loans on the other hand had to be borne entirely by Irish taxpayers – at a rate of 5.7 % for the IMF loan and 6.05 % for the EU loan.

The pressure exerted on the government in Dublin by the IMF, the ECB and the EU on top of the bail-out, requiring it to "clean up" public finances, also helped create conditions that made an economic recovery impossible for years to come.

Thus, the government was forced to sell state assets to international investors at bargain prices in subsequent years. The Burlington Hotel in Dublin, for example, which had been acquired by an Irish property developer for 288 million euros in 2007, was sold to US investment firm *Blackstone* for 67 million euros in 2012, a loss of 77 %. *Quinn Insurance* was sold to US market giant *Liberty Mutual Insurance* – not only at a high discount, but also to the effect that earnings generated in Ireland that were previously reinvested within the country now flowed into the United States. In order to plug more holes in the budget, the government, in agreement with the IMF and the EU, created real estate investment trusts in 2013, which were to provide foreign investors with incentives to become more involved in the Irish property market – another measure that in the long term does not strengthen Ireland's economy, but makes it more dependent on international financial capital, thus laying the foundation for the next crisis.

Many Irish have in recent years experienced a precipitous social plunge, the scale of which no one could have imagined on European soil at the turn of the millennium. The fact that the population, despite the massive deterioration in living conditions, did not rise up in revolt was in large part due to the policies pursued by the trade union leaders. Having made the upswing possible by entering into four social partnership agreements, they showed an amazing willingness to compromise during the boom and were nicely rewarded by the government and by corporations. Their preferential treatment resulted in an even greater decrease of militancy and led to a further widening of the gap between the union leadership and rank-and-file members, who showed their demoralization by turning away from the organizations in droves. While in the early 1980s, 62 % of Irish workers had still been unionized, the number had halved to 31 % by 2007.

After in June 2010, union leadership even gave its consent to the 'Croke Park Agreement', which committed workers to a renunciation of strikes, whatever resistance was left was finally crushed. Only very few protests against social cutbacks followed, most of them quickly disintegrating and coming to nothing.

Support from trade union leadership spelled considerable relief for the Irish government, for it could now implement its austerity measures in close coordination with the IMF, the EU and the ECB without having to fear any real opposition. Although the bailout was officially planned for a period of only three years, the measures will surely affect the working population for decades to come. The "accommodations for payment" that Ireland was granted in the meantime because of its delicate situation show how far into the future the burden to be borne by the taxpayer extends:

While the interest rate to be paid for EU support, which had initially stood at 5.83 %, was lowered to 3.5 %, its term was extended to 15 years. The issuance of long-term government bonds in February 2013, through which the Irish Central Bank, which was placed under IMF supervision, took over the debt of the Anglo-Irish Bank, declared insolvent by emergency degree, went even further. By means of these bonds the Irish government has been granted a moratorium of 25 years. The first redemption payment is due in 2038 and will have to be paid by working people who were not even born when the speculative losses of the Anglo-Irish Bank occurred.

Under the supervision of the IMF, which has not closed its offices in Dublin even after the official end of its "rescue operation" and continues to take considerable influence on all decisions, the Irish government will pursue its austerity measures for years to come and thus deepen the social divide in a country where in 2012, senior bank executives reaped an average annual salary of 1.4 million euros, the 17 highest-paid among them received bonuses of 235 % of their salary, and the number of billionaires has doubled between 2008 and 2013.

The Euro Crisis and the Troika:
Placing Europe under Forced Administration

During the IMF's intervention in Ireland, there was rapidly emerging evidence of a critical development in other countries in the euro zone, especially in Southern Europe. The bail-out of banks following the US mortgage crisis had cost several hundred billion euros and ripped huge holes into the coffers of European states. Some economically weaker countries, such as Greece and Portugal, reported initial cases of payment default, while others showed signs of rapidly increasing problems. It soon became clear that individual problems could easily escalate, thus initiating a Europe-wide conflagration.

The pace at which the situation deteriorated confronted the IMF's leaders with a fundamental question: Should they, in case of emergency, let the countries affected – particularly smaller countries such as Portugal and Greece – exit from the euro zone and return to their old currency, thus allowing them to devaluate massively? In Ireland, the IMF had not seriously taken such a measure into consideration, due to the scale of Irish debt and because of the enormous consequences of a currency changeover. However, since the entire European monetary zone was at risk now, the time had come for taking a fundamental and far-reaching decision.

Various crisis scenarios were played through and yielded an alarming result: Even small countries such as Greece and Portugal had amassed debts to Western European banks amounting to tens of billions of dollars. Since these banks were reinsured by US banks on the basis of credit default swaps, an exit from the euro zone by the countries affected could have triggered a chain reaction that would not only have threatened the existence of the *European Monetary Union*, but that of the entire global financial system. In an attempt to counter this threat, IMF leaders decided to take a landmark decision: No EU country should be allowed to leave the currency union; retaining the euro was declared a top priority.[42]

With the help of the media, this strategy was euphemistically presented to the public as a measure for keeping up the European ideal, securing peace and preventing the disintegration of a continent that was at least bound together by a common currency. In reality it was nothing but the desperate attempt to rein in the effects of the euro crisis and to prevent a global crash by all means.

For the IMF, the decision meant that it no longer had the instrument of currency devaluation within the euro zone at its disposal. Since at the same time it became known that the total amount of debt of the euro countries ranged in the hundreds of billions, the Fund's strategists had to act quickly. They unanimously decided to adopt drastic measures and devised an austerity plan for Southern Europe, which was based on the experience gained in Ireland, but in its harshness and unwillingness to compromise was rather reminiscent of the "shock therapy" the IMF had enforced in the former Soviet Union and the Eastern Bloc. Among others, it called for the following measures:

• To auction off state assets and state-owned companies to the highest bidder in order to promote privatization even without currency devaluation.

---

[42] Germany had called for a sovereign debt restructuring mechanism for countries at risk at the beginning of the debate, but, coming under pressure from the US and the remaining countries of the euro zone, had dropped its demands.

Objections were made that only low yields could be obtained in this way, and that the economies would in the long term become even more dependent on foreign capital, making them even more prone to crises. They were categorically rejected. The only objective was to enable the countries to repay their debts to international creditors as quickly as possible.

• To reduce unit labor costs by significantly sharper intervention in the labor market than before in order to increase the competitiveness of the economies concerned.

For those employees who did not lose their jobs, this meant an increase in the pace of work, fewer breaks and shorter holidays, the deletion of holiday and Christmas bonuses, a reduction of safety standards at the workplace, no additional payment for overtime, abolition of all special services such as child care or other operational benefits, and a suspension of sick pay in case of illness.

• To lay off public sector workers, limit hiring of new workers, abolish tenure, lower starting wages and drastically reduce wages of those who were allowed to keep their jobs in order to reduce the ratio of government spending to GDP – that is, the share of state and state-related economic activities to the overall economic performance of the economy.

The area worst impacted by the reduction of the government-spending-to-GDP ratio was that of social spending. As the unemployed, the sick, the socially disadvantaged, pensioners and children are usually least able to defend themselves and can therefore be expected to put up least resistance, these groups were singled out and targeted first. Furthermore, public institutions such as libraries were to be closed, schools and universities to be merged and their staff reduced to a minimum. Public sports and cultural facilities were to be privatized and shut down wherever no buyer could be found. Hospitals were to be sold into private hands or, wherever this was not possible, to be streamlined and no longer run on the basis of clinical need, but solely based on economic efficiency.

152 In short, the standard of living of the working population was to be re-duced to a level the European continent had not seen since World War II. The authors of the strategy knew very well that besides its extremely negative impact on people's lives the measures would also lead to a significant deterioration of the economic situation of the countries affected, driving them into a downward spiral for years and probably entailing even more and stricter austerity measures. Therefore, they were also aware that the implementation of their measures would pose considerable problems.

The biggest cause of concern for those responsible was the danger of social unrest. The EU, after all, was a highly industrialized zone whose working population had attained one of the highest living standards in the world following World War II. Although it had stagnated for some time and was actually being eroded, even the poor in the less affluent countries of Central and Southern Europe did not have to go hungry; homelessness was only a relatively marginal phenomenon, epidemics were largely exterminated, and basic medical care was guaranteed at least in cases of emergency.

The proposed austerity program would call many of these achieve-ments into question and therefore definitely meet with fierce resis-tance. Protests of considerable proportions were to be expected. The police and the military would probably have to resort to violence and restrict democratic rights, which in turn would lead to popular upris-ings that might threaten the existing order.

The second issue of concern to the IMF related to the governments of the states that were to undergo austerity programs. Although the financial crisis of 2007/2008 had shown that social democratic and socialist governments would not hesitate to pass bank debt resulting from speculation on to the tax-paying population without reservations, even bypassing parliaments and laws, a crucial question remained: how long would people follow them? Given the scale of the austerity measures it was highly probable that large parts of the population would turn away from these parties. However, as their leaders wanted to remain in power or be re-elected at all costs, they could be expected to implement austerity programs either only half-heartedly or by delaying some of the stricter measures, thus jeopardizing their success.

153

The third cause of concern related to the scale of the funds required. According to various estimates, they ranged between 200 and 600 billion euros, thus by far exceeding the financial resources of the IMF. Although the Fund had often intervened as a credit intermediary in the past, sums such as these were impossible to raise on international capital markets, given the significant risks within the euro zone. So what was to be done?

The IMF once again decided to draw on the wealth of experience it had gained in Ireland and recalled that it had found two valuable allies there. The EU and the ECB had unreservedly placed themselves behind its demands and had helped implement the measures required in a relatively short space of time. Both organizations had tremendous financial resources at their command and, by their sheer size and power of wealth, could not only exert pressure on individual EU member states, but also compel them to impose almost any measure required.

The three organizations entered a historic alliance under the name of "Troika" and immediately took up work to complete a task that was without parallel in Europe's history: Forcing the working population in more than a dozen countries, bound together by the same currency, to pay for the damage that had been caused by a tiny minority of financial speculators in an unprecedented orgy of personal enrichment.

To understand the historical role of the Troika, it is necessary to take a brief look at the history of both the EU and the ECB. Their origins go back to the post-war period when Germany, France, Italy, and the Benelux countries (Belgium, Luxembourg, and the Netherlands) joined forces and formed the *European Community for Coal and Steel* (ECSC) in 1951 and, based on the Treaties of Rome, founded the *European Economic Community* (EEC) and the *European Atomic Energy Community* (Euratom) in 1957. In its initial stages the US government actively supported the creation of a bulwark against the Soviet Union and the economies of the Eastern bloc during the Cold War by strengthening the European economy through the establishment of a customs union and by enabling free movement of capital and labor. Germany, which was strongly rebounding after its defeat in World War II, benefitted from the inflow of cheap labor from Southern Europe (euphemistically dubbed as "guest workers" by the media) that led to a boom in the development of its domestic industry and helped improve its competitiveness towards the emerging economies of Southeast Asia in the 1970s and the 1980s.

Between 1973 and 1986, six more countries (Great Britain, Ireland, Denmark, Greece, Spain, and Portugal) joined the community, which from 1967 on called itself *European Community* (EC). The Schengen Agreement provided for the opening-up of mutual borders by all participating countries, while ordering external borders to be sealed off more effectively and impeding or stopping exchanges with countries that were not members of the EC.

In the 1980s, prompted by globalization and increasing financialization of the world economy, leading representatives of major European industrial corporations founded the *European Round Table of Industrialists* (ERT), which became the most powerful lobby group on the continent, exerting considerable influence on the future policy of the EU. The ERT contributed significantly to the deregulation of financial markets in Europe, the drafting of the Maastricht Treaty, the creation of the Economic and Monetary Union and the Lisbon Agenda and repeatedly used its economic power to break the resistance of individual governments against its strategic decisions.

Several key political milestones marked Europe's further development at the beginning of the 1990s. The reunification of West and East Germany helped the country become the most powerful economic force and the politically determining factor in the EU, while the end of the Soviet Union and the reintroduction of capitalism in the Soviet bloc created vast new opportunities for international capital.

155

"Eastward expansion" (the integration of former Eastern Bloc countries into the EU), which was immediately initiated, provided Western financial capital with new markets, while giving the manufacturing industry access to a cheap and highly skilled workforce. Starting in 1993, these workers were also allowed to settle in the core countries of the EU. Although promoted as a measure in support of the "free movement of people", this legal provision had nothing to do with humanitarian considerations. On the contrary, the government-supported influx of cheap labor was used to exert competitive pressure on workers within the EU and resulted in a decline in real wages in the EU by 4.5 % between 2000 and 2009. It also contributed significantly to the creation of a low-wage sector, which since then has continuously expanded and nowadays accounts for more than a quarter of the labor market in the EU's economic powerhouse Germany.

For the new countries of the East, integration into the EU spelled disaster. It led to a higher outflow of capital to the West, a massive brain drain, and the erosion of social systems. Also, disadvantages in relation to the West were deliberately made permanent, as seen in agricultural policies. It was exactly in this area in which Eastern European countries were capable of competing with EU members that their funds were cut in 2000.

The introduction of the euro in 2001 was accompanied by extensive media campaigns designed to make the working population of Europe believe that a common currency would improve living conditions and guarantee lasting peace in Europe. In truth, its main effect was to provide the economically stronger countries with considerable advantages over weaker competitors. Germany, for example, could from that time on escape future appreciations of the Deutsche mark and keep its focus on expanding its export economy. For the economically weaker EU countries, the common currency above all signified greater dependence on the leading nations. Being less competitive in many areas, the euro exerted considerable pressure on the level of their commodity prices and wages. At the same time, working people in Southern Europe had to accept significant cost increases in consumer goods, particularly in food, and permanently come to terms with the alignment of price levels with economically stronger countries of the north.

The "Lisbon strategy" adopted in 2006 was broadly based on Germany's so-called *Agenda 2010*, a legal package which had been implemented by the Social Democrats and the Green Party between 2003 and 2005. It led to the introduction of *Hartz IV* legislation (comprising drastic cuts in unemployment and social benefits) and to the decomposition of the free public health system in Germany. Under the pretext of transforming the EU into "the most competitive and dynamic knowledge-based economy in the world" by 2010, the Lisbon Treaty was used to lower corporate taxes, soften dismissal protection, render labor market laws more flexible und to press ahead with the expansion of the low-pay sector.

The history of the EU shows that its reputation of being a peacekeeper and a motor of prosperity, which has been promoted by the media for decades, is nothing but pure fiction. The EU was and is an organization controlled by the economic interests of finance capital and big business. It has paved the way for an unprecedented accumulation of wealth at the top end of all European societies, while leading to a continuous decline in living standards at the lower end. Half a century of European unification has resulted in a process of fast-growing social inequality, both within individual countries and between the various countries of Northern and Southern Europe. Instead of creating the foundations for lasting peace, the EU's policy has led to its exact opposite: By increasing social inequality, it has laid the ground for severe social conflicts and created the conditions for future disputes between states.

By creating the Troika, the IMF allied with an organization that repre-   157
sented the same interests that it stood for itself. The EU was not only
able to provide money for the loans needed, but due to its size and
power could exert massive pressure on individual governments and, in
case of emergency, even bring them down. The fact that the IMF and
the EU could rely on the ECB, thus establishing the monetary policy
of individual central banks and in case of need directly intervening in
financial markets by buying up government bonds (which, though illegal, was – and is – common practice) provided the tripartite alliance
with a wealth of power that was unprecedented in times of peace in
Europe.

As neither the members of the EU's main executive body (the European Commission), nor those of the Executive Board of the ECB, nor
the officials of the IMF are elected, but rather appointed by different
panels that are hardly known to the public, the Troika is not only one
of the most powerful organizations, but also one that is not democratically legitimized by the people of Europe. Although its establishment
has not abolished parliamentarism on the continent, it has de facto
disabled it, de-activating basic forms of democratic control, thus paving the way for subjecting the continent to the direct and undisguised
dictatorship of the most important bodies of international finance
capital.

Greece and the Troika:
Bringing Hunger back to Europe

At the end of October 2009, newly elected Greek Prime Minister Papandreou declared that the country's budget deficit for the current year would be more than twice the amount predicted by the predecessor government. Greece would by no means be able to meet the budget deficit limit of 3.7 % of GDP demanded by the EU.

The troika made up of the IMF, the EU and the ECB responded immediately, taking control of the Greek budget and imposing the toughest austerity program the country had seen since the end of the military dictatorship in 1974. Among other things, it provided for a reduction in government spending by 10 %, budget cuts in health care, an increase in various taxes, a raise in the retirement age by two years, and job cuts and wage reductions in the public service.

In April 2010, even before the measures could take effect, the government in Athens turned to Brussels for help, conceding that the country's financial situation was much worse than admitted until then. Greece was unable to repay overdue loans and needed financial aid to avert national bankruptcy.

Following Ireland and Spain, Italy and Portugal also reported increasingly critical economic and financial data at ever-shorter intervals, prompting those responsible in the Troika to realize that a crisis of immense proportions was looming. Upon closer inspection, it soon became clear that previous measures would not suffice to combat it. Also, since the monetary union had only been established in 2001, there was no earlier experience to be drawn on. So what was to be done?

The IMF, the EU and the ECB engaged in extensive consultations and came to a far-reaching conclusion: Greece was to become their test laboratory. The country was relatively small and manageable and therefore suitable for a social experiment, which would be conducted with the aim of finding answers to the following questions: How far would it be possible to go in enforcing austerity programs within the euro zone? At which point would the population start rebelling against spending cuts, wage cuts and the elimination of social programs? When would people begin to put up a fight? By what means could civil resistance be undermined most effectively and how could a civil war be averted?

In order to immediately counter any rejection of this test program by the working population in other countries of the euro zone, a media offensive was launched pursuing only one objective: To thoroughly discredit the Greek people in the eyes of their neighbors. Europeans were told that Greeks had lived beyond their means for decades, that a lot of them were social spongers, unwilling to work, and that the country therefore had to be subjected to severe austerity measures. Greece's economy was said to be shadowy, pervaded by tax evasion, bribery and kickbacks. Beyond that Greeks were accused of having obtained membership in the euro zone by presenting false balance sheets and forging statistics.

The first allegation was completely unfounded. Average Greek income in 2009 was at the lower end of the euro zone, with only Portuguese workers earning less. Minimum wage in Greece was 4.05 euros per hour. 20 % of the population had an income below the poverty line, 60 % of retirees had to make ends meet with less than 600 euros a month. The average salaries in the public sector were around 1,200 euros.

As regards the second charge, if anyone was to blame for tax evasion in Greece, it was certainly not the common people but only small layers of the upper middle class and the ultra-rich, most of whom, however, hid their fortunes in offshore havens with the support of major international banks, thus evading taxes by entirely legal means. Notable bribes were mostly paid by foreign corporations and did not flow into the pockets of Greek wage earners, but went straight into the wallets or foreign bank accounts of corrupt government officials, politicians, or managers.[43]

161

The charge that Greece had fraudulently acquired euro zone membership was actually justified, but again, it was not the working population that was to blame. It was the political leadership of the country that had turned to US investment bank *Goldman Sachs* years earlier when Greece had been incapable of meeting the basic entry requirements for the monetary union. *Goldman Sachs* had agreed to grant Greece a loan of 2.8 billion euros, albeit not at market rates, but in the form of highly speculative derivatives swaps (a bet on rising interest rates). Through the use of a notional sum of 15 billion euros (which increased the fee for *Goldman Sachs* many times over), the US bankers and the government in Athens had jointly succeeded in officially reducing Greek debt by 2 %.

The bet on rising interest rates, however, did not come off and a second bet that was frantically arranged, was also lost. In the end, however, Greece was actually allowed to join the euro zone on the basis of its fraudulent documentation, but at the cost of 5.1 billion euros. While the politicians involved in the fraud protested their innocence, presenting themselves as victims of financial maneuvers which they "did not understand", the bankers of *Goldman Sachs* returned to the City of London with a fee of $ 800 million in their pockets. (Their former

---

[43] During the European election campaign in 1999 for example, the German *Siemens* Corporation paid 1 million Deutsche marks to the PASOK party in support of its industrial policies and its strategy of privatization.

boss of European risk management, Mario Draghi, denies to this day that he knew anything about the deal with Greece). Once again, it was the Greek taxpayers who lost out, being left behind with an additional

162   debt of 5.1 billion euros that has to be paid off until the end of 2020.

Accusing the Greek people of having lived "beyond their means" in the years before the outbreak of the crisis was not only absurd, but also a complete distortion of the facts. While the collaboration of politicians and *Goldman Sachs* bankers had led to a higher debt burden, the introduction of the euro had contributed to a considerable decrease in the purchasing power of ordinary citizens. It had driven prices of consumer goods to the level of richer countries, boosting the cost of living and leaving many Greeks, whose average income had been comparatively low anyhow, with considerably less money to spend than during the times of their old national currency, the drachma.

Although perfectly well informed about all these facts by their experts, the IMF and the Troika, in return for their first emergency loans, enforced two austerity packages on Greece that were particularly detrimental to low and medium income earners. The first one, implemented in April 2010, provided for the reduction of the salaries of civil servants, the deletion of their 13th and 14th monthly salary, the reduction of administrative costs and a VAT increase to 21 %. The second austerity package, implemented in May 2010, went much further and among other things called for a freeze on civil servants' salaries over 2,000 euros, the closure of more than 600 municipalities, an 80 % hiring freeze in the public sector, raising the retirement age from 61.3 to 63.4 years, a further increase in VAT from 21 % to 23 % and an increase in taxes on tobacco, liquor and fuel.

In early 2011 it became increasingly clear that Greece's financing need was even higher than assumed until then. In February, the EU finance ministers agreed on another "rescue package" with loan commitments of more than 130 billion euros, to which the IMF contributed 28 billion euros in March. In return for the release of the funds the working population had to accept a third austerity package in June 2011 which called for the privatization of state assets worth 50 billion euros, a renewed increase in VAT by 2 %, the introduction of a "solidarity tax", the abolition of tax exemptions and the dismissal of 150,000 public sector workers by the year 2015. In addition to reducing a number of benefits, it included first significant cuts in health care. By 2015, spending in this area was to be reduced by 1.43 billion euros.

In order to monitor cuts, savings and reforms and ensure their enforcement, in September 2011, the EU set up the "Task Force Greece", a thirty-member team of experts headed by Horst Reichenbach, a German economist and member of the German Social Democratic Party. Although not democratically legitimized, the Task Force Greece was equipped with extensive powers, and its representatives were given the privilege of tax immunity.[44]

Events in November 2011 showed to what extent parliamentary democracy had already been undermined in Greece. When Prime Minister Papandreou, whose socialist PASOK party suffered from acute loss of members due to its acceptance of all austerity measures, announced a referendum on further austerity measures, the troika immediately stepped in, cancelling the vote and ensuring that Papandreou was quickly replaced by Loukas Papadimos, the ex-vice-president of the ECB who had been governor of the Greek Central Bank during the introduction of the euro and whose role in the manipulation of public budget finances with the help of investment bank *Goldman Sachs* had never been clarified.

Greece's fourth austerity package, implemented in February 2012, set in motion a social regression no European country had ever experi-

---

[44] Neither the representatives of the troika, nor those of the Task Force have to prove their financial status to the authorities when purchasing real estate, private vehicles, yachts, stocks, bonds or other assets – a procedure which is obligatory for Greek tax-payers.

enced in peacetime. 15,000 public employees were laid off with immediate effect; the salaries of the majority of the remaining staff were cut by 20 % retroactive to the beginning of the year. The minimum wage for adults was reduced to 586 euros for adults and to 525 euros for young people. Unemployment benefits were reduced to 322 euros, old-age pensions were cut by 10 % to 15 %, co-payments for pharmaceuticals increased, medical services in hospitals reduced, and remuneration for overtime by doctors was cancelled.

164

As this head-on attack on the living standards of ordinary people coincided with constantly changing news about escalating bankers' bonuses, a huge capital flight abroad and gigantic capital gains of the super-rich, anger among working people increased significantly. Tens of thousands of unemployed, pensioners and young people took to the streets in protest in Athens, Thessaloniki, and other cities. Politicians reacted with police crack-downs. The media rushed to the aid of the state, slandering justifiably outraged victims of austerity as rioters and terrorists. In order to discredit the protests abroad and stifle any burgeoning solidarity, the media in other European countries also stepped up their campaign of slander.

Led by the German tabloids, Greek workers were portrayed as lazy southerners, refusing to work, barely paying taxes, happy to retire early in life in order to collect disproportionate pensions. IMF head Christine Lagarde herself contributed to the campaign by suggesting that "Greeks should pay their taxes", thus presuming a Greek mentality of tax evasion. (She failed to mention that her own income as a member of a UN organization, amounting to about $ 50,000 a month, excluding fees and expense allowance, is exempt from all tax payments.)

Politicians of all hues willingly contributed to the smear campaign. German Chancellor Angela Merkel alleged that multiculturalism was dead and claimed that whoever accepted German help was in return expected to make appropriate "efforts", thus ascribing scrounger mentality and a lack of diligence to Greeks. Merkel even went as far as accusing European taxpayers of unknowingly contributing to the idleness of Greek workers by providing them with "rescue" packages.

Even a cursory glance at the credit tranche released by the European Stability Mechanism (ESM) in June 2012 illustrates the absurdity of this statement: Of the 18 billion euros stemming from the euro bail-out package and going to Greece, 6.9 billion euros went to the National Bank, 5 billion euros to *Piraeus Bank*, 4.2 billion euros to the EFG *Eurobank Ergasias* and 1.9 billion euros to the *Alpha Bank*. Not a single cent of this alleged "aid payment" benefited the working population in Greece.

Despite the continuing deterioration of the economic situation and even with the recession entering its fourth year, the Troika did not even consider dropping any of its demands. While thousands of small businesses had to be shut down, almost every other young person lost their job facing long-term unemployment, and while homelessness and drug addiction were spreading, the IMF, the EU and the ECB unbendingly stuck to their policies, enjoying the full support of the media.

In March 2012 a "haircut" was presented to the public by politics and media as an almost humanitarian act of financial markets towards a country on its knees. In reality, Greece's debt which had been reduced by 107 billion euros with private creditors, rose by exactly those 130 billion euros which had been approved in the IMF's second "rescue package" and which in the years ahead will have to be repaid by Greek taxpayers, including interest and compound interest. The "haircut" thus did not reduce the debt burden, but rather increased it.

Its experiment in Greece taught the IMF and the troika an important lesson with regard to further interventions within the framework of the euro crisis. Despite increasingly tougher austerity measures and initially violent protests against the government, the opposition of the working population continued to subside, in many cases giving way to a mixture of resignation and hopelessness. There were two reasons for this: On the one hand, many Greeks turned their backs on the established parties which they had initially hoped would stand up and fight for them, and on the other hand, many were deeply disappointed because of the futility of trade union protests.

In October 2009, the social democratic PASOK party had still been able to win the parliamentary elections by an absolute majority. Many of their followers even kept supporting them when the PASOK leadership broke almost every promise they had made during the election campaign. However, when they allied with the Troika and finally supported the enforcement of the most severe austerity measures, a large part of the working population turned their backs on them. The same was true – albeit to a lesser degree – for the trade union confederations GSEE and ADEDY. Although they had called more than a dozen general strikes during the crisis, they had always limited them to one or two days, thus deliberately rendering them ineffective.

It did not escape the rank-and-file members' attention that union leadership, despite criticizing individual measures, basically accepted the politics of austerity and, while the crisis kept deepening, showed less and less willingness to put up a fight. They also noticed that the unions' top officials preferred to meet with the political leaders of the country behind closed doors rather than openly convening with their own members, and that they only called strikes when pressure from the grass-roots level threatened to get out of hand.

When even the imposition of martial law against truck drivers, bus drivers, ferry and train staff did not prompt union leaders to change course, more and more working people realized that the strategy and tactics of their leadership, instead of serving the interest of the rank and file, was instead aimed at defusing their anger by randomly mobilizing them to blow off steam, thus turning their protests into entirely fruitless performances leading to nothing.

Just as in Ireland, events in Greece thus revealed a global trend that had been observable on all continents over the past decades: the widening gap between leaders and members of trade unions. Due to the continuously growing pressure exerted by financial markets, the trade unions' room for maneuver had been restricted further and further, particularly during collective bargaining, strikes and mass layoffs. As a result, union leaders more and more frequently opposed the demands of the rank and file, in many cases openly collaborating with business and politics, and moving to the right politically.

167

Proceeding from the assumption that no serious resistance had to be expected from the unions, the Troika imposed two more austerity packages in November 2012 and in March 2013 that amounted to a declaration of war on the welfare state. On top of all previous measures, the retirement age was raised to 67 years across the board, old-age pensions of more than 1,000 euros were reduced by 5 % to 15 %, wages and salaries in the public service slashed by as much as 6 % to 20 %. Christmas bonuses for pensioners, as well as Christmas and holiday pay for employees in the public service were abolished. Severance pay in case of dismissal was reduced, and child benefits for families with an annual income of more than 18,000 euros were cancelled.

Higher co-payments for drugs and an "admission fee" for in-patient care[45] in hospitals were added to the sweeping reforms that had already been implemented in health care. Due to long-term unemployment, 30 % of the Greek population were no longer covered by health insurance and had to pay for their health care out of their own pocket. While Greek billionaires could easily afford to be treated in the world's most luxurious clinics, uninsured women were forced to pay three monthly average wages for the delivery of a baby in a hospital – or give birth at home. To this day Greek children can only be vaccinated

---

[45] The "admission fee" was introduced in January 2014. Due to fierce protests it was abandoned that same month.

for cash. Due to their desperate financial situation, thousands of pensioners, unemployed and homeless people are forced to do without vitally essential medication. Unable to afford professional help, many of them have to bear unnecessary suffering, and even expect an early death.

Germany in particular played a crucial role in these reforms. During the course of the crisis, the Troika instructed the Task Force Greece and the German Federal Ministry of Health (BMG) to reduce the Greek health budget to a level of 6 % of gross domestic product, almost half of the 11.3 % that Germany spends in this area.[46] By having the BMG call in companies such as *KSB Clinic Consultation, B & K Computer Science and Consulting*, and the German development agency GIZ and by completely subordinating Greece's health care system to the principle of economic efficiency, the Greek health budget, which in 2009 had still run at 14 billion euros, was reduced by 4.5 billion euros, i.e. almost one third, to 9.5 billion euros in 2012.

This policy resulted in the closure of 46 out of 130 hospitals, accompanied by budget cutbacks of 40 % for the remaining hospitals, and the layoff of 26,000 staff in the health sector, among them 9,100 doctors. This in turn resulted in an increase in the suicide rate by 40 %, an increase in the number of HIV-infected drug users by more than 2000 % from 2008 to 2013, the spread of malaria, tuberculosis, West Nile and dengue fever. The most shocking figures are likely a 19 % increase in the number of low birth weight children between 2008 and 2010, a 21 % increase of stillbirths between 2008 and 2011 and the increase in child mortality by 43 % between 2008 and 2010.

Despite the devastating effects of their policies, neither the Federal Ministry of Health in Berlin, nor the troika even thought of questioning their strategy. Instead of concerning themselves with the fate

---

[46] Reducing the costs for the health system in Germany to 6 % of GDP would mean cutbacks of around 160 billion euros.

of malnourished or dying children, officials preferred to devote their time to the development of Greek government debt in relation to gross domestic product. This figure actually increased steadily in complete disregard of all austerity measures. Having risen to 157 % in 2012, it reached 176 % in 2013 and was predicted to climb to 192 % in 2014.

Austerity policies thus threatened to miss their official main target: the sustainable reduction of public debt, by which Greece was to be enabled to settle its financial liabilities to the IMF, Western countries, banks, and financial institutions in the long term. The Troika had to realize that previous measures were insufficient, and that it had to immediately develop new, more ambitious and even harsher methods of raising money.

But how was this to happen in a country where real wages of the working population had already been reduced by more than 40 %, two thirds of young people had been driven into unemployment, and whose economic power and consumption capacity had been destroyed for years to come? The experts discussed various options and played through a variety of scenarios until an idea gradually evolved that had already been discussed during the Asian crisis in the mid-1990s. It promised access to a new source of money, but also went far beyond all previous measures, bringing with it a significant problem: Its implementation in a country with more than eleven million people could lead to financial and social shocks that might spread across Europe and set the continent on fire.

While the leaders of the Troika were still discussing the risks of such a daring move, the government of the third-largest island in the Mediterranean in March 2013 suddenly captured their attention. Cyprus, which in June 2012, following Ireland, Greece, Spain and Portugal, had been the fifth country to apply for aid in the euro zone, was facing increasing difficulties that demanded a quick solution.

The timing of Cyprus' call for help could not have been better for the strategists of the IMF, the EU and the ECB. With a population of less than a million, its economic power only at 0.2 % of the euro zone and a banking sector that had 32 billion euros in deposits from non-EU citizens, the country was a perfect temporary replacement for Greece as the troika's laboratory, thus serving as a starting point for a test which was to elevate the meaning of the term "shock therapy" to an entirely new dimension.

Cyprus and the IMF:
After Looting Comes Expropriation

Owing to its geographic position in the Eastern Mediterranean, Cyprus has always been of particular geostrategic significance as a gateway between Europe, Africa and the Middle East. Still, for centuries, the country had only played a minor role in Europe's economy. In the mid-1970s, the government in Nicosia decided to change that situation.

The corporate tax was reduced to 10 % and accession taxes and taxes on stock market profits were abolished in an attempt to lure foreign investors into the country. Several international ship owners actually had their fleets registered in Cyprus, and, due to the Lebanese civil war, a number of wealthy Lebanese opened up accounts with local banks between 1975 and 1990. The overall success of the measures, however, remained rather limited.

A major turnaround occurred when the USSR collapsed in 1991. The small layer of oligarchs that had evolved from the pillaging of Soviet public property soon began to look for a place where they could safely invest their billions. Attracted by low taxes, discreet public authorities, a pleasant climate and the fact that 50,000 Russians were already living there, many of them opted for Cyprus.

The Cypriot government subsequently did everything in its power to please its affluent clientele and turn the country into a center of international finance. It facilitated the purchase of real estate for foreign investors, generously handed out residence permits and made natural-ization easier for wealthy applicants. In 1996 it set up a stock exchange in Nicosia, and from 1997 on allowed foreigners to own 100 % of Cypriot companies.

Capital flowed into the country to such an extent that Cyprus' financial sector almost exploded. The number of financial holding companies[47], which had amounted to less than one thousand in 1995, increased to 40,000 by 2000. At the same time Cyprus' industrial production and agriculture were grossly neglected, leading to a loss in competitiveness, thus making the country even more dependent on foreign investors.

The EU observed developments in Cyprus suspiciously as the banks of the euro zone were missing out on a profitable business. Unwilling to merely look on any longer, the EU changed its strategy at the beginning of the new millennium, offering the Cypriot political leadership membership in the EU and access to the monetary union without continuing to insist on unification of the separate parts of the country which had been divided in 1974.[48] The government in Nicosia agreed, and in 2004, Cyprus became a member of the EU without its northern territory, which remained occupied by Turkey. In 2008, Cyprus introduced the euro.

When Greece was drawn into the euro crisis in 2009, its problems soon spread to Cyprus. Being its largest trading partner and importing

---

[47] Financial holding companies are investment companies that do not produce goods themselves, but, as umbrella organizations, dominate financing, planning and the development of all associated enterprises.

[48] In 1974, parts of the military seized power in a coup aimed at unifying Cyprus with Greece.

The Turkish army responded by occupying the northern part of the island. The Turkish Republic of Northern Cyprus was proclaimed in 1983. To this day several ten thousand Turkish soldiers are deployed in the northern part of Cyprus.

more than 20 % of its products, Greece's recession brought the GDP in Cyprus down by 1.9 % in 2009. The austerity measures dictated by the Troika exacerbated the economic downturn and increased unemployment and indebtedness of private households and small businesses not only in Greece but also in Cyprus. The close interdependence of the banks of both countries proved to be particularly harmful. Major Cypriot banks, the size of their balance sheets now four times as large as the GDP, had granted approximately 40 % of their loans to Greece and consequently suffered a wave of increasing loan losses.

In order to be able to continue paying generous interest on their customers' assets, Cypriot banks in 2010 and 2011 bought huge amounts of Greek government bonds – a substantial part of them from the *Deutsche Bank*. For a while this seemed to minimize the problems, because Greece, downgraded by the rating agencies due to its deterioration in credit-worthiness, had to pay extraordinarily high interest on its bonds. (It turned out later that the sole beneficiary of the deal was the *Deutsche Bank*.)

In June 2011, a devastating explosion occurred on a naval base in Southern Cyprus in which the main power plant of the island was completely destroyed. The repair costs tore an additional hole of nearly one billion euros into the state budget. Closely cooperating with the EU, the government drew up an austerity program aimed at cutting the budget by 750 million euros. It provided for a two-year freeze in public sector wages, cuts in social benefits for employees, an increase in the capital gains tax as well as an additional tax on annual income exceeding 60,000 euros and an increase in VAT from 15 % to 17 %. When the measures were announced, they caused such public outrage that the demand for raising VAT was dropped.

The next shock followed in October 2011. Greece and the Troika jointly agreed on a haircut for bond owners in the amount of 53.5 %. While those in charge at *Deutsche Bank* in Frankfurt rubbed their hands in glee, having sold off their Greek government bonds in time, the two largest Cypriot banks had to cope with losses of 4.2 billion euros. A wave of protests throughout the country and increasing criticism of the close cooperation between politicians and the Troika caused the political leadership of the country to distance itself from the Troika, publicly criticizing it and boycotting individual measures.

This in turn aroused the interest of the political leadership in Moscow, which at that time had two good reasons for trying to improve relations with the Cypriot government. On the one hand, the future of the only Russian naval base in the Mediterranean, located in the Syrian port of Tartus, was threatened due to the tense situation in Syria. Moscow's leadership therefore had a strong interest in replacing the base by getting access to the ports of Limassol or Larnaca in Cyprus. On the other hand, rich natural gas deposits had recently been discovered in the Eastern Mediterranean that attracted the attention of Russian energy companies. In order to keep all options open, Moscow took advantage of the situation and in December 2011 granted the government in Nicosia a bilateral loan of 2.5 billion euros at a preferential interest rate of 4.5 %.

Although the agreement between Cyprus and Russia was a deliberate affront to the Troika, the IMF, the EU and the ECB accepted it with a great sense of calm, knowing that Russia's financial resources in the long term would not suffice to rescue a country whose troubled financial sector now covered total assets of over 150 billion euros. Also, the leaders of the IMF, the EU and the ECB were thoroughly convinced that they had the necessary means at their disposal to force the recalcitrant leadership of the smallest euro zone country to its knees whenever they considered it appropriate.

Subsequent events soon confirmed the Troika's assessment of the situation. While Cyprus' financial position continued to deteriorate, the EU raised the capital guidelines for Cypriot banks to 9 %, thus triggering financing requirements of 1.8 billion euros for the Cyprus Popular Bank alone, which had to be covered by mid-2012. When the Cypriot government once again turned to Moscow for another loan, the ECB, which had supported the Cypriot banking system by providing several billion euros within the framework of the Emergency Liquidity Assistance (ELA), intervened, announcing that due to their downgrading by the rating agency Fitch, Cypriot government bonds would no longer be accepted as collateral within the euro zone – a measure they had not even taken in the case of Greece.

Thus, Cyprus was cut off from international capital markets, and resistance from the government in Nicosia was broken. The leadership of the country had no choice but to ask the Troika for help and thus clear the way for the economic and social disintegration of the country. The international media once again told a different story: Although the Troika itself had forced Cyprus to accept the bailout, the media created the impression that it had "intervened in a helping manner" and was negotiating with the government to get Cyprus back on its feet financially.

A cash check subsequently carried out showed that Cyprus's financial situation was considerably more threatening than previously thought. Balance-sheet totals of the banking sector were now almost eight times the GDP; gross national debt stood at 87 %. Also, the balance sheets of Cypriot banks included private and corporate loans to banks in Greece amounting to at least 22 billion euros. Even conservative estimates put preliminary funding requirements at around 15 billion euros.

The figures clearly showed that all previous recovery programs had reached their limits. Tax increases, wage cuts, cuts and redundancies in the public sector did not suffice to meet the funding requirements in a country with a population of less than one million. Furthermore, following Ireland, Portugal, Greece and Spain, Cyprus was already the fifth of 17 euro zone countries that could not free itself from the weight of its debt by domestic means. Rescue costs had meanwhile reached a total of 1.6 trillion euros, a sum that was far beyond anything anybody had imagined at the beginning of the crisis. By establishing the European Stability Mechanism (ESM), which began its work in mid-2012 and was to replace the European Financial Stability Facility (EFSF) as of mid-2013, the EU had already set up the largest bank in the world with a common capital stock of 700 billion euros. The fact that public debt in Greece and Spain alone amounted to 1.4 trillion euros, twice the ESM capital stock, showed how big the gap between the financial needs and the resources allocated to its coverage had already become.

Basically, the financial world was on the brink of stage three of the global crisis, which had been triggered by the collapse of the subprime mortgage market in the United States. Stage one had seen the imminent collapse of "systemically important financial institutions" being averted through the use of taxpayers' money. Stage two had witnessed the attempt to plug the resulting holes in state budgets by imposing austerity programs on the working population. Now stage three made it increasingly clear that austerity alone was insufficient to raise the necessary sums. In order to stabilize the global financial system, a new source of money had to be found.

For some time, international financial circles had been discussing where the required funds might come from. In 2010, the *Bank for International Settlements* (BIS) had published a White Paper in which a model was put up for discussion which was to be applied "in case of future banking crises" and for which the experts had already invented a new name: bail-in. In contrast to a bail-out – i.e. rescuing insolvent banks using taxpayers' money – a bail-in calls for shareholders and creditors of a bank to participate in its losses. In other words, ailing banks should no longer be saved by involving the state but by directly accessing the assets of small shareholders and savers.

The Financial Stability Board (FSB), which since 2009 had been monitoring the global financial system on behalf of the G20 and which counted the IMF among its members, immediately embraced the idea of the BIS. In July 2011, headed by its first director Mario Draghi, at that time also Governor of the Italian Central Bank, the FSB published a consultation paper on the topic of bail-ins, entitled "Effective Resolution of Systemically Important Financial Institutions", which already contained very detailed proposals for the implementation of bail-ins. Among other things, it proposed "issuing new company shares without shareholder consent through an accelerated procedure" and "overriding the right of pre-emption by shareholders when liquidating a company".

177

Switzerland, seen as a pioneer in matters of financial regulation in Europe, acted without delay. On September 1, 2011, the Swiss Financial Market Supervisory Authority (FINMA) announced "revised reorganization provisions" of the Swiss Banking Act which regulate the "conversion of deposits into new equity capital ... to maintain systemically important functions in the event of a crisis", thus laying new legal foundations providing that to rescue ailing banks, recourse is to be taken to the assets of small shareholders and savers instead of turning to the state for help.

The IMF also took up the issue and published a discussion paper entitled "From Bail-Out to Bail-In" on April 24, 2012. On the hypocritical pretext of "protecting taxpayers from exposure to bank losses", the experts of its legal department and its money and capital markets division drew up a highly sophisticated plan for the mass expropriation of depositors, small shareholders and holders of bonds.

The savage clarity in which the paper assessed the situation of the global financial economy was striking. While IMF leadership used every opportunity to spread the tale of an "economic recovery" in order to calm down the international public, the paper bluntly stated: "The potential risks posed by systemic financial institutions for financial stability have increased", and "the degree of concentration of the European and the US financial sector is higher than ever before, thus aggravating the too-big-to-fail problem." The paper also conceded that "the shadow banking system which has played a crucial role in the emergence and spread of systemic risk is still under-regulated".

178

The paper went on to give a step-by-step description of how to carry out bail-ins and also clearly stated how the IMF planned to deal with the legal matters: "There are compelling arguments for a course of action that reduces the role of the courts. Given the need to act quickly and to put restructuring decisions in the hands of managers with the necessary technical expertise, it would seem reasonable to have these decisions made by the banking supervisory authorities."

Precisely this paper was to serve as a textbook for the Troika's strategy towards Cyprus, which, due to its isolated location, its small population and a share of only 0.2 % of the economic power of the EU seemed perfectly suitable to replace Greece as its new test laboratory. By early 2013, an action plan had been drawn up which laid down the following provisions: The government in Nicosia was to be granted a loan of 10 billion euros. Nine billion were to come from the ESM, one billion from the IMF. The interest rate was fixed at 2.5 %; repayment of the loan was scheduled for a period of 12 years from 2023 until 2035. In return, the Cypriot government was to wind up the country's second largest bank, force the largest bank to assume the second largest's liabilities to the ECB, and give its consent to a drastic austerity program, that was to be complemented by a bail-in in the amount of 5.8 billion euros.

The austerity program, aimed at reducing the state budget by 351 million euros, called for reducing public sector wages by 6.5 % to 12.5 %, lowering pension benefits by 3 %, introducing new property taxes expected to yield 70 million euros, raising the corporate tax from 10 % to 12.5 %, increasing taxes on tobacco, alcohol and fuel, raising the value-added tax from 17 % to 18 % in the current year and to 19 % the following year, raising the taxation of interest earnings from 15 % to 30 %, and finally privatizing several state enterprises. The bail-in plan provided for a 6.75 % compulsory levy on bank deposits of less than 100,000 euros and a 9.9 % compulsory levy on deposits of more than 100,000 euros. The implementation of the measures was to be accompanied by the temporary closure of banks.

This new austerity program was the hardest head-on assault on the working population of any country to date, not only within the EU, but worldwide. Therefore it was no surprise that the government in Nicosia kept delaying its consent on the flimsiest of pretexts. The Troi- ka initially put up with its delaying tactics in order to give Western banks the opportunity to withdraw their fixed investments. Then, in March 2013, the Troika clearly demonstrated who called the shots in Cyprus, applying the thumbscrews to the country's political leadership by threatening to end emergency cash assistance to the Cyprus Popular Bank – a move that would have inexorably led to a disorderly sovereign default.

A few days later the government in Nicosia gave in and announced its acceptance of the austerity program, simultaneously ensuring that no major electronic transactions could be made and that no sums of more than 400 euros could be withdrawn from ATMs. The result was an outburst of anger the likes of which the country had not seen for decades. As of March 15, thousands took to the streets, besieged government buildings and protested so vigorously that the government was compelled to postpone a parliamentary debate planned for March 17 for safety reasons.

On March 18, protests gained such momentum that the government tried to calm things down by promising to exempt small investors with accounts of less than 20,000 euros from the scheme. On the night of March 19, the parliament finally came together. The result was a slap in the face of the Troika. Not a single member of parliament voted in favor of the measures, 36 voted against and 19 abstained.

Furious about such rejection of their conditions, the officials of the IMF, the EU and the ECB began to openly talk about excluding Cyprus from the euro zone. Fearing a bank run, the Cypriot government ordered an extension of the bank closures until the end of the week and limited the amount of withdrawals at ATMs to 100 euros. Then it made one last attempt to escape a bail-in, bringing up the idea of a rescue fund based on gold reserves, church-owned capital and money from the pension fund which was to be legally authorized to issue government bonds. The Troika responded by announcing that it would cut the emergency line of credit for Cypriot banks as of Monday, March 25, if the Cypriot government continued to refuse meeting their demands.

On Friday, March 22, German Chancellor Angela Merkel intervened, warning Cyprus sharply to stop testing the patience of the Euro countries. The Cypriot Parliament responded by giving in and agreeing to large parts of the rescue plan that same day. Two days later, the Cypriot president traveled to Brussels to attend a special session of euro zone finance ministers. On the night of Monday, March 25 – before European stock exchanges opened for the week – an official agreement was reached. It corresponded largely to the demands of the Troika without exactly specifying the conditions of the bail-in. Only one detail was released immediately: deposits of less than 100,000 euros in the Bank of Cyprus were to be spared, while those above 100,000 euros would have to contribute a projected maximum of 40 % of their assets to the cost of a rescue operation.

In order to win over the European public and to conceal the true meaning of the bail-in, the Troika immediately launched a media campaign that portrayed Cyprus as a refuge for illegal earnings from Russia and presented the bail-in for assets above 100,000 euros as a morally justified act of taxation of Russian oligarchs. Just how little this had to do with reality became obvious for the Cypriot people on March 28, when the island's banks, guarded by the British security firm G4S, reopened after having been shut down for 12 days. Due to capital controls they were not allowed to withdraw more than 300 euros per day from their accounts or transfer more than 2,000 euros per month abroad. Issuing or cashing in checks was prohibited with immediate effect.

For Russian oligarchs, however, such obstacles did not exist. As the public was to learn later, they were given the opportunity to transfer money abroad via the London branches of the two Cypriot banks – without limits for transfers and throughout the entire period of the bank closure. As the *Bank of Cyprus* held a stake of 80 % in the Russian *Uniastrum Bank*, transfers to this bank were also possible without any limitation. The fact that the Russian government promised the EU full cooperation in the restructuring of banks in Cyprus after the final adoption of the rescue plan suggests that Brussels and Moscow had come to an arrangement behind the scenes. The ECB's public warning to Latvia not to let Russian money into the country as that would threaten its acceptance into the euro zone may well be seen as an attempt to deliberately divert attention from the money flows to London and Moscow.

Russian oligarchs, by the way, were not the only ones who succeeded in transferring their fortunes to safety in time. Wealthy British individuals also used the transfer option to London, while Greek ship owners had already deposited their assets with the Norwegian bank DNB in preceding months. As the central bank governor later admitted, "better-informed" investors (by which he mainly referred to German and French banks) had already transferred more than 10 billion euros abroad in 2012.

The final bail-in was announced in late April and provided for losses amounting to 80 %, thus doubling the initially announced 40 %. More than 60,000 small investors that had turned their savings into bonds of the two major banks lost almost everything. Among them were many owners of small and medium-size businesses that were now unable to raise the money they urgently needed to keep their companies going. Those affected to the worst degree by far were the Cypriot workers, whose standard of living had been drastically reduced by the bail-out package, and who were now facing decades during which they would have to bear the burden of higher debt and lower income, at the same time being forced to put up with a largely defunct and continually disintegrating social system.

182   The main beneficiaries of the Cyprus crisis were undoubtedly the major European banks. For years, especially German and French banks had been able to borrow money at low rates from the ECB and invest it at interest rates between 2.8 % and 4.9 % in Cyprus. After the onset of the crisis, the Troika willingly accepted the stalling tactics of the Cypriot government from 2012 until 2013, thus providing the banks with the time they needed to avoid the threat of a bail-in and move the bulk of their funds, including gains, out of the country. This drying-up of the Cypriot banking system caused many enterprises to transfer their banking to larger Western European countries.

Also, billions of dollars of mainly Russian investors were transferred to Western banks, helping these banks meet their increased demand for cash. For the major financial centers of New York, London and Zurich, the destruction of the Cypriot financial sector also meant eliminating a competitor and thereby strengthening their global position of power.

Western companies were also among the winners. On the one hand, they were able to purchase medium-sized businesses which had run into financial difficulties at rock bottom prices and use unemployment, which had risen to 15 % at the beginning of 2014, in order to put pressure on wages and reduce production costs, thus making these enterprises "internationally competitive". On the other hand, the privatization program obliging the government to sell state property such as the electricity company AHK, Cypriot telecommunications and the two most important ports of the country, Limassol and Larnaca, by 2018 in order to raise 1.4 billion euros to meet its liabilities, offered (and still offers) them great investment opportunities.

The oil and natural gas reserves in the Aegean Sea have also become the focus of attention for several Western corporations. By early 2014, 15 major companies from 14 countries, including the US, France, Italy,

Australia, Russia, South Korea and Malaysia had submitted official requests for exploitation rights. Awarding the rights to foreign multinational corporations as part of its privatization program will ensure that hardly a cent of the 600 million euros the reserves are estimated at will go to the impoverished working people of Cyprus, but that instead, the lion's share will flow straight into the pockets of ultra-rich international investors.

The IMF after Cyprus: Institutionalizing Theft

The way a bail-in works is basically as simple as it is perfidious: a group of investors makes money with a bank until it runs into payment problems due to the speculative activities of its management. When it comes to raising the necessary capital for a financial restructuring of the bank, it is not the investors that are asked to touch the profits they have amassed over the course of years. Neither are the managers responsible for bad speculation held liable for the losses. It is the depositors, savers, and small investors – those who have nothing to do with the business policies of the banks – who are forced to cough up some of their deposits and ultimately look on powerlessly as their money – which they believed to be safe – is passed on to investors. By implementing such measures, the state does not only adopt the role of an institutionalized thief, it also channels the money workers have earned into the hands of the very individuals who caused the problem in the first place by entering into transactions that were too risky, thus ensuring that the carousel of speculation can continue its rounds even after the banks in question cease operations.

The IMF's tenacity in following this policy is demonstrated in the case of Cyprus. At no point did it intervene in order to exempt depositors with accounts of less than 10,000 euros from the bail-in. Instead, it even demanded their 6.75 % share in the measure in accordance with the Troika. The fact that this scheme was not put into practice was due exclusively to the Troika's change of course. Faced with angry protests by large sections of the population, it backed down, no longer insisting upon its demand, albeit for purely tactical reasons.

Nonetheless, the international financial industry was still satisfied with the solution in Cyprus. Right after the implementation of the bail-in, the Institute of International Finance (IIF), the most powerful lobby organization of the finance industry, announced that "the approach in Cyprus... could very well become a model for dealing with collapses elsewhere in Europe" and that "investors would be well-advised if they saw the results in Cyprus... as an image of future stress management."

The USA, as well as Canada, Great Britain, Australia, and New Zealand hastened to follow the Swiss example and immediately made arrangements to incorporate the bail-in principle into their legal systems. Furthermore, in a joint paper entitled "Resolving Globally Active, Systemically Important, Financial Institutions", the *Bank of England* and the US *Federal Deposit Insurance Corporation* (FDIC), which insures American bank deposits, proposed that a portion of the sums thus forcefully expropriated be converted into bank bonds, making depositors stockholders to a limited extent. What on the surface appeared to be a compromise was in reality nothing but a clever move aimed at depriving depositors of the possibility of a legal appeal, a juridical option in Anglo-American law.

For the EU, the Cyprus bail-in ushered in a new stage in the management of the euro crisis. Since it was foreseeable that the means of the ESM would not be sufficient in the long run to constantly rescue new banks from collapse, the responsible committees in Brussels immediately got to work incorporating the bail-in principle into the EU guidelines as quickly as possible.

News of this caused unrest in the financial markets in the early summer of 2013. Numerous banks feared that small depositors could empty their accounts before a legal regulation went into effect, thus possibly setting off a bank run. Jeroen Dijsselbloem, president of the Euro Group (the EU committee that coordinates the tax and economic policies of the euro zone countries), therefore turned to the public, denying the plans, and referring to Cyprus as "a special case with unusual conditions." In complete disregard of his statements and behind the backs of the public, the jurists of the EU continued their preparations for a legal regulation.

On August 1, 2013, the EU finally passed a guideline – without debate or a vote by the EU parliament, but supported by the bank representatives of the International Swaps and Derivatives Association (ISDA). It states that "banks with reported capital shortfalls must ensure that shareholders as well as holders of subordinated debt securities make an appropriate contribution to cover the capital requirements before applying for state recapitalization or measures to protect their impaired assets."[49]

The EU had indeed worked quickly and efficiently. Not even six months after the bail-in in Cyprus, the involvement of depositors was legally stipulated throughout Europe. One of the main problems with the European economy seemed to have been solved, as the banks of the 17 euro countries were holding a total of 860 billion euros in unsecured deposits that could now be used for bail-ins. However, a few days before the passage of the guideline, dark clouds passed between Brussels and Frankfurt. A short while later, a conflict that had been brewing for a while between the ECB and EU openly broke out.

Its cause lay with the EBA (European Banking Authority), which was planning a stress test for European banks in 2014. It was quite possible that a few banks would not pass the test and would therefore have to boost their equity. Since according to the guideline of August 1st, savers and creditors of a bank would be first in line having to contribute to its rescue, the ECB worried that upon the first application of the

---

[49] "Subordinated" creditors should be understood primarily as small depositors and small shareholders, whereas "prior ranking creditors" are official institutions such as banks, agencies, or financial organizations that remain spared from the bail-in.

guideline, investors would break out in panic and leave the euro zone in masses.

188   For the EU, however, the bail-in regime primarily meant a relief of the ESM. In particular, Germany as the strongest economy in the euro zone with the highest guarantees in the ESM, insisted that in the event of an increase in equity of a bank, creditors and investors were to be burdened before charging the ESM and along with it the German government.

The difference of opinion between the EU and the ECB fundamentally reflected the dilemma in which the European financial economy found itself in the fall of 2013. At 66 trillion euros, the total balance sheet of the banking sector had grown to four times the economic output of the continent. In order to save the system in the case of a crash, sums would be required that went far beyond what states or depositors could provide. Both measures – bail-out and bail-in – were in the long run nothing more than patchwork and at best able to temporarily stabilize the system. The greatest problem was that beyond those two possibilities, there were no further options on the table, at least until October 9, 2013, when the IMF put another one forward with a bang.

In a 100-page report as part of their publication *Fiscal Monitor* (launched in 2009), entitled "Taxing Times", the tax division of the IMF undertook a meticulous study of global tax policy. Accompanied by dozens of statistics, the paper gave an overview of the development of international tax revenues since the crisis of 2007, and put forward sober economic data. The total debt of the euro states had reached 8.6 trillion euros, the average public debt ratio in all countries in 2014 was approaching the historical all-time high of 110 % of the GDP. Europe was about to exceed its debt level of 2007, i.e. before the financial crisis, by more than a third.

Halfway through the paper, on page 49, there is a section of just 15 lines entitled "A One-Off Capital Levy?" where it says: "The sharp de-

terioration of the public finances in any countries has revived interest
in a "capital levy" – a one-off tax on private wealth – as an exceptional
measure to restore debt sustainability. The appeal is that such a tax, if
it is implemented before avoidance is possible and there is a belief that   189
it will never be repeated, does not distort behavior (and may be seen
by some as fair)."

If one leaves aside the extremely vague formulations and filters out
the actual essence of the text, it describes a compulsory levy upon
private wealth which has the following features: first, those affected
cannot evade it; second, they believe it will only be levied once; and
third, after implementation, they will not attempt to withdraw their
assets or move them elsewhere (for example, abroad). In the further
course of the paper, prominent representatives of such an idea from
the history of economics are listed, and its chances for success described as "strong."

After pointing out that the measure must be weighed against the risks
of the alternatives – a state haircut on debt or inflation – the paper
mentions a "surprisingly large amount of experience" to which one
can refer. The final paragraph states: "The tax rates needed to bring
down public debt to pre-crisis levels, moreover, are sizeable: reducing
debt ratios to end-2007 levels would require (for a sample of 15 euro
area countries) a tax rate of about 10 % on households with positive
net wealth."

The worldwide effect of the text was as if a bomb had dropped, and led
the IMF to publicly distance itself from it within a few days. An IMF
spokeswoman referred to it as a "purely theoretical thought experiment," and pointed out that the second paragraph even contained a
critique of the compulsory levy. However, even a cursory glance at the
second paragraph was enough to convince anyone that this was not
true. The paper merely established that in the past the levy had failed
primarily because "the delay in introduction gave space for extensive
avoidance and capital flight." In other words, the text did not criticize

the levy in itself, but rather pointed out weaknesses in its implementation.

190 That "Taxing Times" was in no way a pure intellectual experiment is also proven by the passage in which the "large amount of experience to draw on" is historically documented. The authors remind the reader that "such levies were widely adopted in Europe after World War I and in Germany and Japan after World War II," thus making it absolutely clear that the text is not a fruit of someone's active imagination, but based on the experiences of Realpolitik.

Thus, the IMF proposal for a compulsory levy was anything other than a coincidence. As with the bail-in proposal of April 2012, it was a carefully planned action to steer public discussion in the direction desired by the IMF. Those responsible had expected outraged reactions and deliberately used them to provoke critics into blowing off steam, while at the same time making the public familiar with the idea of a compulsory levy.

The IMF proposal also contained a tiny footnote that referred to a paper by the Deutsches Institut für Wirtschaftsforschung (*German Institute for Economic Research*, known by its German acronym DIW) of 2012, in which the economist Stefan Bach had demonstrated that a one-time compulsory levy of 10 % could raise about 230 billion euros. However, there was a decisive difference between the DIW proposal (which was later retracted) and that by the IMF: in his paper, Bach made an exception for assets under 250,000 euros, and only proposed to apply the levy to the wealthiest 8 % of the population. There is no mention of any restriction of this kind in the IMF text.

Another noteworthy item in "Taxing Times" was the declared goal of the measure of "reducing debt levels to end-2007 levels." The authors did not even try to create the illusion of tackling any kind of problem, such as the crisis in health care and education or youth unemployment. The sole aim of the proposed introduction of the compulsory levy was to turn back time and recreate conditions that had existed six years prior.

Since not a single truly significant measure has been taken since the crash of 2007 to limit the power of the banks or restrain the international casino of capitalism, the effects of the compulsory levy described by the IMF were not difficult to predict: it would allow the state to appropriate part of the financial means of ordinary people – their savings accounts, small stock portfolios, savings to educate their children, retirement provisions – and place them at the disposal of those who would, without any inhibitions due to the lack of legal regulations, feed them straight back into the cycles of speculation in order to continue to voraciously enrich themselves without regard for the social consequences.

Mountains of Debt, Social Inequality, Revolution: Ringing in the End of the IMF?

According to the international media, the world has been undergoing an economic and financial recovery from the crash of 2007 since 2011. Journalists throughout the world spare no effort to constantly detect new signals for an upward trend and present them to the public as proof of the "sustainability" of the recovery.

At the same time news media have been flooded by reports according to which the international financial system stands at the edge of the abyss, its final crash being only a matter of days or weeks. The international book market has seen the emergence of a veritable "crash" industry in which prophets of doom serve an audience of millions with their more or less apocalyptic predictions.

The fact that both phenomena are able to exist side by side can only be explained by the nature and the uniqueness of the current situation. It is the result of a development that has no precedent and does not fit into any existing scheme. Yet nothing could be further from the truth than assuming that the world economy is on its way to recovery. Quite the opposite: All of the measures that have been taken since the onset of the financial crisis in 2007 in order to stabilize the system have, without exception, helped undermine and weaken it, making it even more vulnerable and unstable in the long term.

The global debt burden, which was at $ 70 trillion in 2007, had grown to $ 100 trillion by the middle of 2013. Wherever the banks encountered legal limitations, they shifted their activity to the opaque network of the shadow banking system, which, according to cautious estimates, exceeded a sum total of $ 21 trillion in Europe alone. Along with a massive overabundance of speculation, the fear of inflation has led to a situation where material assets serve as a "safe haven", heating up global real estate markets and causing massive price bubbles. Unrestrained lending to emerging markets may prove to be the most dangerous development. In complete disregard of the experiences of the crises in Latin America and Asia in the 1980s and 1990s, large international banks doubled their loans to these countries between 2008 and 2013. At the beginning of 2014, the indebtedness of the emerging markets reached a breathtaking $ 9.1 trillion.

These numbers leave no doubt: the dangers lurking in the global financial economy have not declined, but rather increased to a considerable extent. They also show that the financial sector has not become more restrained or cautious as a result of the crisis. On the contrary: the large financial institutions have not engaged in less risky behavior since 2007, but rather indulged in greater risks than in previous years. No wonder, since due to their designation as "systemically important" and "too big to fail," large international banks have obtained a special status that has never before existed in economic history. It is true that businesses have also been rescued from ruin in the past, but declaring an entire branch to have permanently become an indispensable component of the global economy, thus making it practically untouchable, was and is without precedent in history.

Before 2007, there was a line in the sand for even the most aggressive among the investment banks that kept their willingness to engage in risky behavior in check: fear of bankruptcy. For banks declared "too big to fail," this line no longer exists. They can enter into any kind of risk conceivable without having to fear their own end. They can even, as the past few years demonstrate, willfully position themselves above the law without those responsible being held accountable. The criminal practice of selling financial products while at the same time betting against these products, the illegal manipulation of foreign exchange, the revelation of the Libor scandal, the multiple police raids on the top management of banks, and the numerous prosecutions against bankers that were terminated in favor of monetary fines in Frankfurt, London, Zürich, and New York[50]: all of these are just the tip of the iceberg. Politicians have effectively issued a group of people a blank check that allows them to indulge in any kind of behavior, no matter how unscrupulous.

The consequence is that the three most important trends of the last few years have not only continued, but have accelerated: the concentration of economic and financial power in the hands of a constantly declining number of firms, the concentration of a greater amount of wealth in the hands of a tiny group of super-rich individuals, and the dismantling of the rights of the general public in favor of an increase of privileges for a diminishingly small minority.

According to a study by ETH Zürich, 1.7 % of multinational companies now control 80 % of global transactions, 147 companies alone control 40 %. As regards private wealth, matters do not look any different: about 5 % to 10 % of the wealthy share 80 % of the wealth worldwide. But not only these figures alone are are breathtaking, but also the speed these trends have gathered in the last few years: worldwide, the number of billionaires has shot up from 793 in 2006 to 2,170 in 2013. Between 2009 and 2013 alone, 880 people advanced into this group, and an increase of 250 each year is prognosticated for the period up to 2020. The wealth of the super-rich has more than doubled between 2009 and 2013, from $ 3.1 trillion to $ 6.5 trillion.

The result of this fast and furious development is an unprecedented rise of the most critical indicator of any human society: social inequal-

---

[50] US regulatory agencies alone have levied fines of more than $ 100 billion upon large American and foreign banks, due to illegal activity for the period up to 2014, more than half of which is for activity in 2013.

ity. Never before were the differences between the extremes so great as today. In 2013, 85 of the richest individuals in the world owned assets amounting to $ 1.7 trillion, a level of wealth equal to that of 3.5 billion people, or half of humanity.[51] In Great Britain in 2013, five families owned as much wealth as 20 % of the population. In India in the same year, 56 families possessed total wealth equal to 500 million of their compatriots. The richest man in the world, the Mexican telecommunications mogul Carlos Slim, would have been able to pay the annual wages of 440,000 Mexicans from his interest earnings alone. The contradictions are most severe in the USA, where in 2013, there were 500 billionaires in contrast to 50 million people who were dependent upon food stamps to survive.

While millions of people at the lower level of society have been driven into abject poverty by neoliberal austerity programs, its upper level has witnessed the greatest orgy of self-enrichment in the history of humanity. In a world in which 840 million people go hungry, 770 million have no access to drinkable water, just as many cannot read or write, and 80 million children will never see a school from the inside, a few individuals possess such enormous wealth that they could rebuild the education and health systems of entire states.

This terrifying state of affairs is not only the logical consequence of the current system's manner of functioning, in which making a profit is the goal that overrides any other considerations. It is also an indication of what to expect in the future. As long ago as the third century BC, Aristotle wrote: "Real or imagined inequality is always the occasion for unrest and revolutions by the citizenry." Two centuries later, the Greek philosopher and historian Plutarch said that "an imbalance between rich and poor is the oldest and most baleful affliction of all republics". 2000 years of human history have impressively confirmed both statements. Numerous revolts and revolutions have shown: The

---

[51] The numbers come from a report by the human rights organization *Oxfam* of January 2014.

greater the inequality within a society, the greater the social tensions and the greater the probability that revolts and revolutions will occur.

The neoliberal policies that the IMF has helped promote have led to a situation where we inhabit the most unequal world of all time. In addition, social tensions are increasing at a historically unprecedented pace, and not one of the measures taken in the past few years to manage the crisis has led to an improvement or even a stabilization of the situation. Bail-outs, austerity programs, unlimited money printing, and zero-interest policies by the central banks have worked like distributing heroin to addicts: feigning a temporary state of emergency, while weakening the organism in the long-term. Bail-ins, the compulsory levy proposed by the IMF, and further social cuts will surely come, but their effects will dissipate even more quickly, further eroding and hollowing out the system with relentless consistency.

Working people around the globe find themselves in the midst of an unstoppable and irreversible downward spiral, which continuously lowers their living standards, with every further measure hitting them harder than the previous one. History shows that such demoralizing experience creates and fuels anger that develops its own dynamic. It slowly emerges over longer periods, flares up, seems to disappear, but then spreads under the surface like a smoldering flame in order to explode sometime, ending in revolts and revolutions.

Nobody can say when these social disruptions will occur. But that they will occur is as sure as the fact that water turns to steam when heated. The events in Tunisia and Egypt were the first premonitions. They made clear the proportions that the social anger of desperate masses can take on. They also demonstrated that revolutions can occur in completely unexpected places and develop a dynamic that goes beyond individual countries.

Greece, Spain, Portugal, and other southern European countries have seen countless demonstrations. During some of them, signs with slogans such as "Down with the troika," and "To hell with the IMF" could be read. Most of these protests were forcefully put down just like the uprisings in Tunisia and Egypt. But violent repression does not calm people's anger. On the contrary: it feeds it and causes it to seethe and brew until at some point it explodes unexpectedly.

The concrete form that revolts and revolutions will take in the era of social networks and unprecedented possibilities for communication cannot be prophesied. On the basis of historical experience, however, one can say this: in order to maintain the current system with the support of organizations such as the IMF, governments faced with growing social inequality will be forced to resort to increasingly harsh police state measures. If these fail to keep increasingly violent protest at bay, only two options remain: dictatorship or starting wars.

The darkest periods of the 20th century have shown how nationalist prejudices were systematically stoked and nightmare scenarios were created in times of great economic problems in order to distract people from those responsible for their problems and channel their anger into military conflicts. The rising number of followers of radical right-wing organizations in Europe as well as increasingly noisy saber-rattling by military leaders and their growing willingness to participate in armed conflicts throughout the world are very obvious alarm signals.

In the event that working people, against all odds, one day manage to see clearly through the haze of lies incessantly spouted by the media and politicians, release themselves from the strangling grip of the established parties and organizations, and use the coming confrontations to develop new and contemporary forms of struggle and organization, then they will be able to seize an historic opportunity: to create a new social order on the basis of the most advanced forms of technology and science which will no longer serve to satisfy the boundless greed of a minority, but the social needs of the majority. What exactly such a society will look like only the future will reveal, but one thing can be said for certain: organizations such as the IMF will have no place in it.

THE END

IF ONLY THE WAR ON POVERTY WAS A REAL WAR THEN WE WOULD ACTUALLY BE PUTTING MONEY INTO IT.

Bibliography

»Manias, Panics and Crashes«
Charles P. Kindleberger, Robert Z. Aliber
Palgrave Macmillan, 2011

»A Financial History of Western Europe«
Charles P. Kindleberger
Taylor & Francis, 2007

»The World in Depression, 1929-1939«
Charles P. Kindleberger
University of California Press, 2013

»Capitalizing on Crisis«
Greta R. Krippner
Harvard University Press, 2011

»A Brief History of Neoliberalism«
David Harvey
Oxford University Press, 2007

»The Enigma of Capital«
David Harvey
Oxford University Press, 2011

»Global Slump«
David McNally
PM Press, 2010

»John Maynard Keynes: 1883 – 1946: Economist, Philosopher, Statesman«
Robert Skidelsky
Penguin Books, 2005

»How much is enough? The Love of Money and the Case for the Good Life«
Penguin Books, 2012
Robert and Edward Skidelsky

»The Age of Inequality« in »Institutional Racism and the Police:
Fact or Fiction?«
Robert Skidelsky, Herausgeber: David G. Green
The Cromwell Press, 2000

»Five Years of Economic Crisis«
Robert Skidelsky
Centre for Global Studies, 2014

»Globalizing Capital: A History of the International Monetary System«
Barry Eichengreen
Princeton University, 2009

»Global Imbalances and the Lessons of Bretton Woods«
Barry Eichengreen
MIT Press, 2007

»Exorbitant Privilege: The Rise and Fall of the Dollar and the Future of the
International Monetary System«
Barry Eichengreen
Oxford University Press, 2012

»Thirteen Bankers. The Wall Street Takeover and the Next Financial
Meltdown«
Simon Johnson and James Kwak
Vintage, 2011

»White House Burning«
Simon Johnson and James Kwak
Vintage, 2013

»Pricing Theory, Financing of International Organizations and Monetary
History«
Lawrence H. Officer
Routledge, 2007

»It takes a Pillage: An Epic Tale of Power, Deceit, and Untold Trillions«
Nomi Prins
SWN Books, 2013

»The Alchemists: Three Central Bankers and A World On Fire«
Neil Irwin
Penguin Press HC, 2013

»The Great American Stickup«
Robert Scheer
Nation Books, 2010

»Perfectly Legal: The Covert Campaign to Rig Our Tax System«
David Cay Johnston
Portfolio Trade, 2015

»Financialized Capitalism: Expansion and Crisis«
Costas Lapavitsas
Maia Ediciones, 2009

»Web of Debt«
Ellen Hodgson Brown
Third Millennium Press, 2010

»Superclass. The Global Power Elite and the World They are Making«
David Rothkopf
Farrar, Straus and Giroux, 2008

»Hirten und Wölfe: Wie Geld- und Machteliten sich die Welt aneignen«
Hans J. Krysmanski
Verlag Westfälisches Dampfboot, 2010

»La Banque: Comment Goldman Sachs Dirige le Monde«
Marc Roche
Albin Michel, 2010

»Tatort Zürich: Einblick in die Schattenwelt der internationalen Finanzkriminalität«
Leo Müller
Econ, 2006

»Geheime Goldpolitik: Warum die Zentralbanken den Goldpreis steuern«
Dimitri Speck
Finanzbuch Verlag, 2013

»Debtors' Prison«
Robert Kuttner
Knopf, 2013

»The Body Economic. Why Austerity Kills«
David Stuckler and Sanjay Basu
Basic Books, 2013

»Global Brutal«
Michel Chossudovsky
Zweitausendundeins, 2002

»Globalization of Poverty and The New World Order«
Michael Chossudovsky
Global Research, 2010

»Africa's Odious Debts«
Leonce Ndikumana and James K. Boyce
Zed Books, 2011

»Globalization and its Discontents«
Joseph Stiglitz
W.W. Norton & Company, 2002

»The Price of Inequality«
Joseph Stiglitz
Penguin Books, 2012

»Balkankrieg: Die Zerstörung Jugoslawiens«
Hannes Hofbauer (Hg)
Promedia Verlagsgesellschaft, 2001

»The Shock Doctrine«
Naomi Klein
Henry Holt, 2007

»A Demon of Our Own Design: Markets, Hedge Funds, and the Perils of Financial Innovation«
Richard Bookstaber
Wiley, 2009

»The Great Risk Shift«
Jacob S. Hacker
Oxford University Press, 2008

»Plutocrats: The Rise of the New Global Super-Rich«
Chrystia Freeland
Penguin Books, 2012

»The Big Short. Inside the Doomsday Machine«
Michael Lewis
Norton, 2011

»The IMF and Economic Development«
James Raymond Vreeland
Cambridge University Press, 2003

»Rating-Agenturen – Einblick in die Kapitalmacht der Gegenwart«
Werner Rügemer
Transcript Verlag, 2012

»The Summit: The Biggest Battle of the Second World War –
fought behind closed Doors«
Ed Conway
Little, Brown, 2014

Webseiten

actionaid.org

ag-friedensforschung.de

afrol.com

allafrica.com

alliancesud.ch

boeckler.de

brettonwoodsproject.org

christianaid.org.uk

citizen.org

econbiz.de

equaltimes.org

erlassjahr.de

foodandwaterwatch.org

fondad.org

globalexchange.org

globalissues.org

globalpolicy.org

globalresearch.ca

hdr.undp.org

huffingtonpost.com

imf.org

mit.edu

multinationalmonitor.org

opednews.com

oxfam.org

prokla.de

prospect.org

publiceye.org

retro.seals.ch

rosaluxemburgstiftung.de

suedwind-magazin.at

theguardian.com

therules.org

thirdworldnetwork.net

twnside.org.sg

unesco.org

weed-online.org

worldbank.org

wsj.com

wsws.org

Image Credits: 12 / Harry Dexter White and John Maynard Keynes at the opening meeting of the IMF's Board of Governors in Savannah, Georgia, March 8, 1946; http://commons. wikimedia.org/wiki/File:WhiteandKeynes.jpg // 19 / Camille Gutt at the Bretton Woods conference, 1944; http://commons.wikimedia.org/wiki/File:Camille_Gutt.jpg // 21 / Ivar Rooth (1888–1972); http://sok.riksarkivet.se/sbl/Presentation.aspx?id=6856 // 29 / Augusto Pinochet (left) meeting with US Secretary of State Henry Kissinger (right), 1976, Archivo General Histórico del Ministerio de Relaciones Exteriores; http://commons.wikimedia.org/ wiki/File:Reuni%C3%B3n_Pinochet_-_Kissinger_%282%29.jpg?uselang=de (CC-by-SA 2.0) // 58f. / Christine Lagarde, 2007, photography by MEDEF; http://commons.wiki media.org/wiki/File:Christine_Lagarde.jpg?uselang=de (CC-by-SA 2.0) // 81 / Protest in Seoul (South Korea) against neoliberal structural change, which first began with the IMF's measures in response to the Asian Crisis, October 13, 2008; https://www.flickr.com/pho tos/skinnylawyer/5508238107/ (CC-by-SA 2.0) // 103 / Milton Friedman (1912–2006), undated, The Milton Friedman Foundation for Educational Choice, http://commons.wiki media.org/wiki/File:Portrait_of_Milton_Friedman.jpg?uselang=de (CC0 1.0) // 119 / US President Ronald Reagan and British Prime Minister Margaret Thatcher at Camp David, December 22, 1984, White House Photographic Office, http://commons.wikimedia.org/ wiki/File:Thatcher_Reagan_Camp_David_sofa_1984.jpg?uselang=de // 143 / Dominique Strauss-Kahn, 2007, photography by Marie-Lan Nguyen; http://commons.wikimedia.org/ wiki/File:Socialist_rally_Zenith_2007_05_29_n4.jpg?uselang=de (CC-by 2.5) // 200 / Liberty Plaza, New York City, USA, photography by Sasha Kimel, September 26, 2011, photography slightly cut on the sides (CC-by 2.0)

Licenses

CC-by-SA 2.0: http://creativecommons.org/licenses/by-sa/2.0/
CC0 1.0: http://creativecommons.org/publicdomain/zero/1.0/
CC-by 2.5: http://creativecommons.org/licenses/by/2.5/
CC-by 2.0: http://creativecommons.org/licenses/by/2.0/